Weddings ... I do!

A guide to being a wedding magician

By
Wayne Goodman

Weddings ... I do!

Published by Wayne Goodman Entertainments.
For more copies of this book please email:
wayne@waynegoodman.co.uk
Tel: (+44) 07726 190078
Designed and Set by Wayne Goodman Entertainments

www.waynegoodman.co.uk

ISBN: 978-0-9928201-9-0

Cover Art by WG
Edited by Johnny Toro

CAN'T AFFORD THIS BOOK?
A percentage of every book sold subsidises another for those who cannot afford a copy. If you genuinely cannot afford this book & would like to apply for a subsidised copy please contact wayne@waynegoodman.co.uk

This book is dedicated to my beautiful daughter
Charlee Autumn Mae Goodman
My inspiration

Special Thanks to

Andy Chase
Mollie May
Daniel & David Bean
Simon Shaw

This book would not have been possible without the help of:

My Mum for supporting me all these years through thick and thin.

Christian Fletcher
Peter Nardi
Juan Muino
Fiona and Finn Muino
Graham and Rachel Farnham at Regency Cakes
Julie Donnelly
Lucie Owen-Drawbridge
John Morton
Michael Murray
Dave Bonsall
Sarah Davies
Katharine Edmunds & Family
Eric (El Rico) Armstrong
The Members of the Ipswich Magical Society
Michelle Andrews
Leon Heussen
Scott Paton
Gideon Hall
Luke Jonas
The members of the Group

Plus all the venue staff and wedding suppliers too numerous to mention.

With Thanks

This book would not have been possible without me giving thanks to so many people.

If you know my name, know what I do or have seen me perform at any kind of event.

Then I thank you, you have helped shape me into the magician I am today.

Special thanks must go to:

Claire Trett - Claire appears multiple times in this book in photos etc and if you are wondering which one she is, just check my website she is on every page.

Juan Muino who continues to inspire and push me to be a better performer and wedding supplier.

Peter, Harry and Andy at Alakazam Magic for all their help and support.

The Group. The Group is a select number of friends and magicians who I chat to privately and have been a massive support for myself and each other over some very hard times. A truer group of friends would be hard to find.

Eric "El Rico" Armstrong for all his teachings and advice over the years

Simon Shaw for all his amazing support and kindness over the years.

Andy Chase, Lei and Stan the man for making me laugh and cry and being so supportive with ideas and advice.

Molly May-May for being the best BFF anyone could ever ask for, and for my constant Waynees and Smiles.

Charlee, my daughter and arch nemesis, who inspires me daily and is the only person in the world who can make me laugh so much it hurts.

And finally to every Bride and Groom who has ever trusted me with making their day as magical as it can be.

This book would not have been possible without all of you and I truly am indebted to you all for everything.

Contents

Forward   10

Introduction   11

The Wedding Magician   19

Types of Magic   25

Breaking the States   27

Getting Booked   36

Wedding Fayres   37

Wedding Advertising   66

Website   70

Wedding Suppliers   82

Wedding Venues   91

The Booking   95

The Wedding   106

Attire   111

The Reception   115

The Wedding Breakfast   123

Evening Reception   130

Children at the wedding   133

The Bride and Groom   142

The Magic   147

Magic at the Tables   148

Look Sharp Anniversary Edition   152

AC Deck of Cards   153

WG Deck of Cards   155

The Interaction   157

Diamonds are for Everyone   160

Wayne's Wizarding Wine   165

Horror Stories   169

Jokes   172

Wayne's Wedding Statement   175

Forward

Andy Chase

Firstly I want to say what an honour it is to be asked to write the forward to this amazing book, which in my opinion is not just for wedding magicians but is for all performers or anyone that works at weddings.

Let's start with 'Wayne'! I have known Wayne for over 15 years when he first lectured at my local magic club.

He is a master magician and someone who I have grown up admiring and learning from. The first time I joined the Alakazam Discord (which I highly recommend), I saw Wayne was in one of the rooms, and it was scary to jump in and say 'Hi' to someone who has inspired me and created such amazing effects like 'Look Sharp' and many more.

This was the start of our very close friendship. I don't think a day has passed since we have not spoken, played with ideas or me learning something new. I can honestly say he is one of the most down to earth people I know and one of life's nice guys, as well as being a world class magician. My daughter Mollie-May calls Waynee her BBF and he is an amazing dad to his own daughter Charlee.

Now this book.....
If you are a beginner and looking at starting to perform at weddings or you have already done 1000s of weddings, I promise you there are loads in this book which will help, improve your act, get more gigs and make you think about your role as a wedding magician.

I could say loads about this book, however, I am sure you are keen to just get reading, learning and laughing. I will say Just WOW and thank you Wayne for writing this master class in the Weddings you do!

Andy Chase.

Introduction

Hi and thank you so much for purchasing or stealing this book, I hope you enjoy the information I am about to share with you and if you have read my other books you will know that my forwards have a tendency to be full of information and set the bar for the rest of the book.

I hope this book is no different, and so I thought I would start off with a whole heap of facts and figures and show you that not only are there plenty of weddings out there, but also what kind of market you are tapping into.

The wedding day is, for the Bride & Groom, or as well shall refer to them, the B&G, the most important day of their lives, this is the day they will remember, reminisce and talk about for the rest of their lives.

Before we start looking at why the couple should book you or why you should be doing weddings in the first place, let's look at some wedding statistics.

According to a study by leading wedding industry experts and at the time of writing (April 2021) it seems the average cost of a UK wedding is £21,740.

There were almost no actual weddings during the pandemic of 2020 so the following numbers are based on weddings in 2019.

If you factor in the honeymoon too this can add anything from 800 - £7000 on top of that figure.

Some couples will spend more and some less depending on their own personal situations and budgets with some spending less than £5000 and some costing more than £40,000.

Bridebook and Hitched both did research that showed that the couples they surveyed, on average spent between £10,000 - £25,000 with a whopping 40% of couples spending more than 50% above their initial budget and only 3.5% being under budget.

*"The **British wedding industry** is booming. Over 139,000 small businesses make up this amazing **industry** which employs over half a million talented individuals and is **worth** over £17 **billion** to the **British** economy."*

So the UK takes over £12billion out of an estimated £92 billion worldwide.

I tried to find the most accurate costs for countries around the world but came up against a stormy sea of so many conflicting prices.

I spoke to some people at a few different respected wedding industry research groups and almost all of them gave me these numbers.

This is the average cost of a wedding for

United States	£22,419
United Kingdom	£21,740
Spain	£17,970
Italy	£17,275
Canada	£16,814
France	£13,513
Portugal	£12,822
Mexico	£6,602
Peru	£5,911
Brazil	£5,067

There were 242,842 marriages in the uk in 2017, the official numbers for 2018 - 2021 have not been released yet, which breaks down to approx 5000 weddings a week.

So let's look at what these 242,842 couples are spending all this money on.

I have always said that the three most important things for any wedding couple are:

- Dress
- Venue
- Photographer

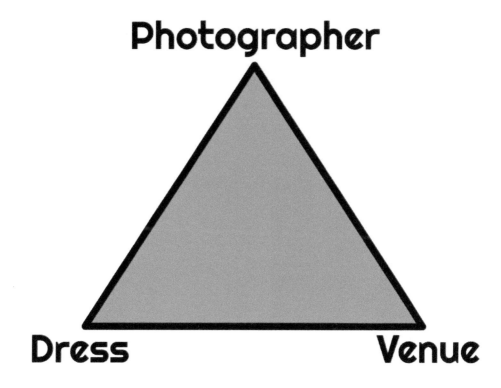

these three items sit atop of the wedding planning pyramid.

Once again according to the time of writing the average costs for these three major items are:

Photographer   £1,155
Dress   £1,313
Venue   £5,406

Remember these are just average numbers and for some wedding items it will depend on location etc.

Now let's look at the next few items that will appear on the planning list.

For 2019 these were the top 10 wedding spends (including the three above)

These items appear in no particular order.

Photographer	£1,155
Dress	£1,313
Venue	£5,406
Honeymoon	£4,645
Mini-Moon	£1,135
Food (if not included in venue hire)	£3,887
Engagement Ring	£2000
Cake	£600
Videographer	£968
Entertainment	£1650

Remember this is the top ten wedding spend list, this does not include vital but not as expensive items such as mens suits, bridesmaids dresses, other outfits, shoes, cakes and stationary.

A lot of money is also spent on pre-wedding events such as stag and hen and engagement parties.

The average that couples spend on pre-wedding parties breaks down as:

Stag	£552
Hen	£472
Engagement Party	£875

And these are just ahead of the groom's suit - £445 and bridesmaids dresses - £344 although it appears that B&G are spending less on gifts for the bridesmaids and best men - £147.

Transport	£700

This is for the basic package and does not include luxury items such as sports cars, classic cars or a tank (yep you can get them).

Flowers   £1300
Most wedding florists will offer a wide selection of flowers and packages but this
came in at the average price for the complete package for the day.

Decorations   £1100

Wedding Cake   £500
This again will depend on what you want and how extravagant you want it.

Shoes   £200

Wedding Stationery   £500

Hair & Makeup   £500

Wedding Rings   £900

Registrar Fees   £300

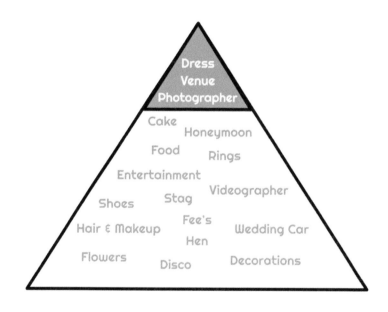

And the list goes on and on and on.

Now aside from the 5 hours of research for me, what does this have to do with magicians at weddings, well amongst all of this was one section that applies to us.

Entertainment £1650

This is pretty much where we live, and this is our small pot of gold that we are trying to get a share of.

This small section now has to be broken down again.

What entertainment do you have at a wedding?

This is not a small question and will depend greatly on the preferences of the B&G however here are some of the more popular choices.

Disco.
Most weddings will have a DJ and Disco and the prices for these will vary from £500 up to £1500.

Band.
Band prices also depend on what you want and how long they are expected to play again with prices ranging from £350 for a solo or two piece to £2000 for a 5 or 6 piece band.

Some bands I have worked alongside will also offer a disco side package (that is already part of their sound system) for between sets and at the end of the night etc.

Children's Entertainers / Carers.
This is not kid's magicians, rather it is normally two or three specialised adults who are brought in to care for and cater for the attention and needs of the children throughout the day, basically a babysitter service.

Caricaturist.
Caricaturists like magicians range in price from £175 - £500.

Musician.
Some B&G will hire a musician to play, including during the ceremony, the reception, the wedding breakfast and even for some parts of the evening. There are many different kinds of musicians who specialise in this field and I have worked alongside many including, a piano/keyboard player, a harpist and even a saxophone player.

Photo booth.
This is something that has become more and more popular over the last 10 to 15 years. Price is normally dependent on time required and number of guests and many companies offer package prices ranging from £300 upwards.

Singing Waiters.
Another modern addition is the singing waiters, I have worked with a few but the best group I ever saw was at a friend's wedding, they pretended to be eastern european and offered to sing a traditional song from their country, it was so funny and really added to the day.

Garden / Outdoor Games.
Classic and giant games like giant Jenga or giant Connect four or just normal games like Quoits or Noughts and Crosses.

Magicians.
Working the reception or around the tables, a cabaret or illusion spot, around the evening reception or just a kids show during the speeches, there are plenty of times a magician is a great addition to the day.

This, as they say, is us.

So a magician can be a key part to the day and depending on how you want to work the day you can arrange a number of packages that suit the individual requirements of every B&G.

I offer a number of different packages and will discuss these later in the book

So from all this we learn that there are a lot of weddings and these weddings happen every

Day - Week - Month - Year

It is a huge market but it is also a huge market place with an equally immense number of wedding suppliers that you are competing against to be seen, however as stated there are hundreds of weddings every day, so there is plenty of room at the table if you can find the right spot for your services.

Over the coming pages and chapters I will share with you everything I have learned about performing at weddings and being a leading wedding supplier in my area.

Wayne Goodman

The Wedding Magician

Like anything in life, it all comes down to the who, the what and the why, so to begin with, let's break down the who, what and why of being a wedding magician.

Who is the wedding magician?
Close up magic has been growing in popularity for years and over the last twenty or so years it has become a lot more prominent at weddings

As close up magic has become more popular, there has been a real shift in the image of the classic magician, gone are the top hats and bow ties, replaced with smart suits or outfits, and a more laid back style of performing.

So who is the wedding magician? Well I believe that like children's magic, stage performers, illusionists or mentalists, the wedding magician's image is defined by the individual performer.

This is particularly important when it comes to weddings, as a wedding is a very personal occasion.

Weddings are deeply personal and therefore a good and successful wedding magician will be one who is open and friendly.

Unlike other wedding suppliers you are not selling a product, you are selling yourself, so you have to make sure you are seen in the best possible way.

Be Yourself.
Being yourself as a performer is the key to any presentation or performance.

If the audience likes you then they will relax and enjoy the show, however, if the audience does not like you they will not relax and this will not help with the atmosphere or your presence around the room.

The main problem is that most magicians who struggle at weddings are the ones who do not realise they are not the stars of the day, they think it is all about them.

You need to be yourself, the B&G have booked YOU, they like YOU and they want YOU, so be YOU but remember it is THEIR day.

Many magicians make the mistake of creating a fake persona to build into a character, then they adopt this character and the real persona as well as the real person, fade into the background.

Know your strengths and weaknesses and play to your strengths. I know I am loud and I am funny so I use these to my advantage when I am in front of a crowd.

If you want to stand out as a performer, then you need to bring as much of yourself to the front and allow yourself to shine.

This is important in all aspects of performance, even if you are an actor playing a part, you should strive to make the character your own.

This is why some great performances are defined by the amazing actors or actresses who portray them.

How often do we hear comments like,

> *"No one else could play Tony Stark.*
> *Robert Downey Jnr made that character".*

That comment could be applied to so many performances from stage and screen as the comments echo each other due to the amazing presence and portrayal that is presented for the audience.

You need to apply this to your own performance, the fake character is that of a magician, but the personality and presentation should be 100% real and 100% you.

What are the wedding magicians' aims?

My main aim is to create a memorable experience, that the whole wedding party will remember, forever!

Being part of a wedding is a huge thing, the B&G are trusting you with their friends and family as well as asking you to be a part of the most special and important day of their lives.

I get so many reviews etc but one of my favorites is this one:

> "Wayne was amazing, he got more attention and comments than my dress and cake".
>
> "He was the highlight of our whole wedding".

This highlights for me that after I had left, I was still being mentioned to the B&G and to others around the room, my job was complete because I had created a sensation and would be remembered for being an important part of the day.

My other aim is to create or exploit situations that can benefit the rest of the wedding day, such as filling the silence and creating a buzz around the room.

Enabling the wedding photographer to capture some amazing pictures of the wedding guests being amazed and in awe.

Creating moments where the wedding guests change from witnessing the events of the day to becoming an actual part of what is happening.

If you take a more indepth look at why you are there, it will enable you to create a deeper and more meaningful connection with the people you are performing for, in whatever show you are presenting.

Why a wedding magician at all?

"Those who don't believe in magic will never find it"
Roald Dahl

Magicians hold a special place in the hearts and minds of most people, everyone loves to watch a good magician perform, and this has been proven quite recently when you watch the viewers choices on any of the Got Talent type shows, where more and more magicians are making it to the finals.

Being a magician who performs at weddings is not only very rewarding and a lot of fun, but it is also a great place to really work some amazing material.

Throughout this book I will describe the benefits of having a magician at a wedding and how you should sell your services to the clients, but this question also resonates with me about what kind of business I have built over the last three decades.

Why do I want to do weddings?
Well, for me, it is easy, I do weddings because it is an almost constant stream of work that I can approach to fill my diary.

Wedding season in the UK is mostly the middle of April - End of October but in reality, weddings happen all year round.

I also love doing weddings because they allow me the freedom to perform multiple genres of magic in one venue.

I can switch and adapt my performance for each and every table I visit.

At one table I am the funniest magician in the world, at the next I am reading minds on par with Professor X and then at the next I am a legend with the kids.

Reflection.
Before we start the main bulk of this book I wanted to add this small section. In my book "Go Compere" I discusses a couple of things that I believe help to define you as a performer, it was in a conversation with my good friend Andy Chase that I should add this section to this chapter.

If you want to work at weddings, if you want to succeed at wedding fayres and if you want to be a star, then you have to have the ability, the skill and the personality that people will be drawn to.

Smile.
It sounds silly when you talk to people and you mention that smiling is one of the most important things you can do when in the spotlight.

Being a magician can be stressful and nerve wracking, you want the audience to like you and a simple smile can move you closer to the goal, do not underestimate the power of a sincere smile.

Tom Wilson said,

"A smile is happiness that you find right under your nose".

A lot of books on body language will tell you the physical and mental benefits to smiling but for the point of view of being on stage I will share just three.

Chemical Happiness.
When you smile, your body releases endorphins, this is a natural chemical in the human body.

This same chemical is released when you work out in the gym or doing any physical exercise, some people refer to this as a "Runner's High".

You can see the effects of this, when someone heckles a politician, or when something goes wrong on stage, the lead person will smile, and when they smile, everyone relaxes because you know that the person in charge will have the answer.

Releasing endorphins also reduces stress and anxiety, so when you are nervous before the show, as you walk out onto the stage, "Smile" and you will feel those butterflies vanish, you will relax and your presentation / act will flow much better.

Smiling releases positive emotions too, that is why we often feel happier around children, they smile a lot, and then so do you.

Smiling makes you appear trustworthy.
You are about to stand in front of a room of people, maybe strangers, maybe your peers and ask them to watch, listen and maybe learn from you.

To do this, whether it is for an act, a presentation or a seminar you have to build trust.

Research has shown that smiling establishes you as a better leader and worthy of trust.

A University of Pittsburgh study revealed people who smile are more approachable, trustworthy and have more likability than people with non smiling facial expressions.

A study at the University of Montpellier, France concluded that smiling is as strong a reflection of leadership qualities as confidence and compassion

Smiling is a gift that spreads.
How many times have you looked at someone and smiled, and they have smiled back? Smiling is like yawning or frowning, it is often referred to as a sign of empathy.

If you see someone frowning, you may also find yourself frowning. Everyone knows if you see someone yawn, then get ready for a yawn yourself.

And it appears that smiling is another that is easily spread. When you smile at the audience, they will smile back at you and everyone feels better and more connected.

"Everyone smiles in the same language."
George Carlin

Types of Magic

A lot of magicians offer a number of different shows for the wedding day.

Close up.
The most popular type of wedding magic and usually done during,

- Drinks reception.
- Wedding breakfast.
- Evening reception.

Make sure you maximise your time at these parts of the day so that you can be seen by everyone, have a good selection of effects and routines and also make use of the fact you can keep your case nearby and change your material throughout the day.

Children's Magic Show.
Most children's shows will occur during the speeches, and used as a way to keep the children entertained whilst the speeches are happening.

However I have seen children's entertainment happening during other parts of the day, including during the daytime reception and also during the evening reception.

I was booked to do close up magic during the daytime reception and wedding breakfast and also provide a children's entertainer and magician for the same times.

A children's magic show can be a real asset to the wedding day and is a great upsell item to add to your package if you are able to perform in this arena.

Cabaret.
Another kind of show that some magicians offer is the cabaret or illusion show, this usually either happens straight after the wedding breakfast or during the evening reception when the evening guests are in attendance.

I have done a number of cabaret shows at weddings, and always find the crowd to be energetic and enthusiastic. The idea of an illusion show has always appealed to me as accommodations could be made to include the B&G in at least one illusion making the day even more special for them.

Choose your performance.
Whichever style you choose to use, make sure you market yourself correctly to the B&G, obviously an illusion act is going to be around 45 mins - 1 hour (unless otherwise arranged), and close uppers will be facing 1 - 3 hours for whatever package they are selling.

If you are not 100% clear about what you offer and what they are buying it can lead to unnecessary and embarrassing situations on the day.

I once did a fake celebrity wedding, there were 45 actual guests for the day and another 20 look-alikes booked to come and have a free meal in character as their alter ego.

Performing magic for Marilyn Monroe, James Dean, Gandhi etc was kinda weird but had a lot of fun and they also had a Tom Jones look and sound alike and a "Only Fool and Horses Grandad" Look and sound alike.

Tom Jones was booked to do a 45 minute set but when he turned up admitted he only did 2 songs, and when the Only Fool and Horses Grandad turned up, he neither looked nor sounded like Grandad at all, which meant most of the audience thought the Groom's actual Grandad was having a go.

Neither of these acts had properly managed or prepared for their booking and were now in a pretty embarrassing situation of trying to sort out, with a quite irate B&G what they were actually able to do.

Breaking The States

Having a magician at a wedding is a pretty normal thing in the UK, but if you head back 25 to 30 years,then it was almost unheard of.

I was shocked to learn that having a magician at a wedding in America and Canada is not something couples do and this made me think of all the areas in the world that are untapped markets for a wedding magician.

This came as a real surprise to me, especially when you consider that in the USA a lot of the culture is based around entertainment and their desire to have big events with plenty of guests.

This chapter does not only apply to countries though, you can look at your own area and see where you can target untapped markets.

For instance, I looked at weddings in my area, I work a lot in my home town of Newmarket, I also work in Cambridge and Bury St Edmunds which are both around 15 mins drive from my home.

I also work a lot in Ely and Thetford to the north of Newmarket but saw I had almost zero shows down towards Haverhill and Saffron Walden to the south.

On the map below you can see Newmarket in the middle of the map with the purple circle around it, and Cambridge and Bury St Edmunds either side of Newmarket with the red circles.

South of Newmarket you can see a number of villages and small towns such as Haverhill, Sudbury, Lavenham, Saffron Walden, Thaxted and Linton.

Within a short time I had identified over 30 wedding venues within one hour of my home that I was not working and made first contact with each of them, firstly to introduce myself as a wedding supplier but also to see about being placed on the recommended suppliers list and if they hosted any wedding open day events or fayres.

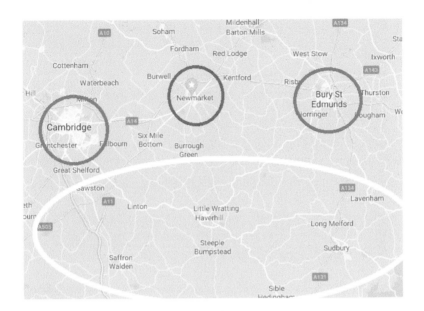

Supply & Demand.

Every salesman knows you have supply and demand, so how do you tap into a sector if there is no demand for it.

Let us again look at North America and the fact that they do not have magicians at weddings, how do we shift the dynamic from zero to 100 percent?

If there is no demand, create demand.

Nobody is going to book a magician for a wedding if they do not think that a magician is correct for the event.

I have come up against this mindset before when I started working at funerals.

So how do you create demand for something when no one is thinking about it?

Well this is not actually that hard if you are willing to spend some time and effort into making it work.

Let's look at a scenario and see how we can make it work.

The Scenario.
You are a magician living in Columbus, Ohio.
You want to start a trend of booking magicians for weddings and break the seal on this untapped market.

Firstly you need to generate a plan of action:

- Research all the wedding venues in the area, at least one hour in every direction.
- Research every wedding supplier who works in the area.
- Find out if there are any locally published wedding magazines.
- Search social media for local wedding groups.

Research all wedding venues in the area, at least one hour in every direction.

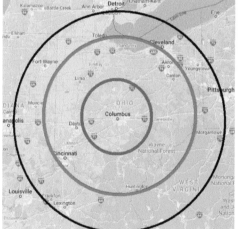

As you can see on the map to the left the purple circle represents 1 hour from the centre of Columbus, with the red being 2 hours and the black being 3 hours.

Find the local venues and see if they are hosting any events to invite B&G's to attend.

Also find out if they have a suppliers list and see if you can get put on the list or the website.

When I first started doing weddings I discovered that one of the venues I regularly worked at for business events was also a wedding venue, this meant that I knew all the staff and they knew me, and knew the standard of service I provide.

Once they knew I was working weddings they started to recommend me and I soon had plenty of bookings coming in.

Research every wedding supplier who works in the area.
Alongside knowing the venues and staff, it is also important to know the suppliers too, these are also people who spend a lot of time talking to potential clients and will recommend and suggest you to them.

You may well already know some of these people as some suppliers such as events teams, caterers etc who you may have worked with before at other events.

Find out if there are any locally published wedding magazines.
This is a great place to find out about wedding events and also teach you about wedding trends etc.

You will soon learn which venues are more popular in some months and less popular in others.

You can start to notice patterns and trends that will enable you to craft specifically targeted weddings advertising.

Search social media for local wedding groups.
This is the goldmine of the modern age, here you will have B&G's themselves asking questions and is a direct point of contact to introduce yourself and the services you offer.

Grab their attention.
So now you have a load of venues and suppliers and you know the wedding magazines and you're tapped into all the social media groups, how do you now grab their attention.

Trends and fashion change constantly, so you need to go big or go home, remember though you only need one person to book you to get the ball rolling, once you are seen at one wedding, other people will want you at thiers.

You need to grab their attention and you need to create some demand, the easiest way to do this is to make them realise they NEED you and NOT having you is NOT a possibility.

In other words, you need them to WANT you.

One technique you can use here is to offer a free show for one lucky couple, put an advert in the magazine, drop flyers at the venues and supplier shops and post in every wedding group.

To view this image full size you can visit: www.waynegoodman.co.uk/book-page

By asking the potential customer to email you to be entered into the competition you should soon start to see people contacting you to find out more about what you do, how it works and can they be added to the list.

Adding a monetary value to the offer also shows you are offering a serious prize, $800 worth of service is something desirable. These people did not even consider having a magician before, but now they are contacting you because they really want to win your services and have you at the wedding.

The B&G have nothing to lose, they could win a free show that will be something no one else has at their wedding, making their day unique and different and all they have to do is email and they are in with a chance.

Allocate each person a number and email it back to them and announce that on a specific date you are going to draw the winner on a live video.

On the day of the draw dress up smart and decide how you are going to choose the winner, numbers in a box that you draw or if you are able to have a screen etc you could go to a random number generator like this one.

www.pickerwheel.com/tools/random-number-generator

You can draw the number and announce the winner live.

Once this is done you can now email EVERY person who entered and did not win and offer your condolences on not winning but let them know that as a thank you for taking part they can still book you for their wedding and also receive a special discount of $200 off the normal fee.

By this point they should really want you at the wedding, the hype is built and they are gutted they lost the competition, but now they are able to still book you and with a discount too.

From a few hours work on social media and posting the competition up etc as well as having people share from my own pages etc and a few flyers printed up and put around my local area I was able to harvest a good number of viable potential clients and their contact details.

Does it work?
I did this very idea when I first started doing weddings and I soon had 40 people signed up for the competition.

I gave one wedding away and was able to book a further 22 weddings from the other couples meaning a conversion of 56.4%.

What additional things do I need to perform at weddings?
If you are already a professional performer then you do not actually need much to be a wedding magician.

- A dedicated page on your website or a bespoke site just for weddings that you can link to your main website.

- A new suit that is just for weddings.

- New business cards and flyers.

You do not need, especially in the early stages, to worry about special routines etc, use the material you are comfortable with, as long as it is appropriate for a family audience, and maybe set aside a couple of effects just for the B&G, also see the chapter on special effects at the end of this book.

Changing minds.
It is hard to sway opinion but also remember that the B&G do not really know what they want, they have a vision of what they want, because of what they have seen at other weddings, but they also want their wedding to be different, more unique and special, and this gives you a huge advantage.

If you can sell the idea of a wedding magician and you are the only one offering this service then you can reap the rewards of the hard work.

A good way to do this just to lead by example, if you're getting married why not book a magician for your wedding.

If you know somebody is getting married then offer to do their wedding for free or even as a wedding gift, this way you are showing the value of the service that you are offering and at the same time giving an example of what you can do.

A lot of comments that I get when I'm talking to B&G's is that they saw something at another wedding and realised that they would like it for their wedding, for example a candy cart, they hadn't considered this before but when they saw it at their friends wedding they knew they needed it too, you need to do the same thing with the service you are offering.

Consider the options of the B&G:

A quick search of my local area and my suppliers list generated these kinds of numbers.

Wedding Supplier	Number of suppliers in the local area
Cake Maker	18
Photographer	23
Wedding Disco and DJ	46
Wedding Venue	28
Venue Decorators	8
Videographers	12
Wedding Planners	23
Magician	3

I know there are other magicians in the area, most are not professional workers and I only have 2 that I would consider good enough for me to recommend to a client for a wedding I could not do.

The B&G have to visit multiple venues to find the one they want.

They have to chat with many photographers and cake makers to make sure that they are getting the service they desire.

The list goes on and on and can be quite draining on the couple, even when it comes to general entertainment in my local area I have 46 disco companies offering packages.

This means when they consider a magician, and the number is very low, the choice is quite easy.

If you're the only magician in your area, and you can sell the idea, then you stand to be the one inundated with the work.

Consider the results.

A new revenue stream which is not only very profitable but does not require a major outlay to accomplish.

A whole new client list that will, if done correctly, lead to more work in other arena's.

A full diary for a major part of the year.

A service that others in your area are not providing, enabling you to be the main service provider for your entire area.

This is not an easy path to walk, you need to work hard and be prepared for everything and anything, but remember that every waterfall starts with a single drop of water and a single drop of water, if moving in the right direction can cause a tidal wave.

If you live in America, Canada or another area that is an untapped market, you could be that tidal wave.

Getting Booked

Getting booked for a wedding means getting known for doing weddings, this is a tricky vicious circle, how can you do a wedding if no one knows you do weddings.

In this first section of the book I will address the key ways to put yourself in front of potential clients and also showing the tools that are available to attract those couples to make contact with you.

Getting gigs has always been a hot topic for any service industry and you will find thousands of discussions detailing ideas and opinions on what is the best way to make it work for you.

I can not say which is right and which is wrong for you and your business but what I can do is tell you what has worked for me, as well as what hasn't worked for me over the last 30+ years in the industry.

Remember also that just because something did not work for me, does not mean it will not work for you, so consider all your options and choose and try the ones that you think will work.

Never be scared to try something new, something daring or something others say will never work, no one knows your business better than you so make a choice, take a chance and if it doesn't work, then you will know to try something else next time.

Ahead of you is a great opportunity to take perform your magic for people on the biggest happiest day of their lives, but it is not an easy option, weddings have a lot of formality and structure that you will need to find your place in, it is hard work but then remember,

"If it was meant to be easy, everyone would be doing it".

Wedding Fayres

Anyone wanting to make direct sales knows you need direct contact with the customer, if you can put yourself in front of the person who is the decision maker then you can make your pitch and sell your product or service.

To do this with weddings you need to put yourself in front of the B&G and what better way than at a one stop shop for all things weddings, a wedding fayre.

A wedding fayre is not dissimilar to a magic convention, there are stands and shows, talks and demonstrations but instead of magic dealers it is full of different wedding suppliers.

With the exception of huge national event wedding shows held at places like the O2 or the NEC (National Exhibition Centre) etc, most wedding fayres happen in hotels, wedding venues or local conference centres.

This is usually dictated by who is organising the wedding fayre and what venue they select to hold the fayre.

For myself I have one large wedding fayre held twice a year and then 5 or 6 smaller fayres that I attend.

The large fayre hosts around 200 wedding suppliers and has a fashion show, make up demonstrations and a car show.

The smaller fayres, normally hosted in wedding venues or hotels, has approximately 20 - 40 wedding suppliers and does not normally host any shows or demonstrations.

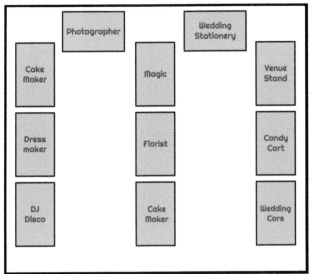

This is a wedding fayre floor plan from one of the small venues I regularly attend.

The layout is one room out of three rooms that have stands in and as you can see the suppliers are evenly spread around the room.

Duplicate suppliers like the cake maker are placed apart.

The idea is that couples and families will attend the fayre and walk around the room starting at one end and visiting each stand as they travel.

This of course does not always happen to plan but most couples visit almost every stand.

The position of your stand is important.

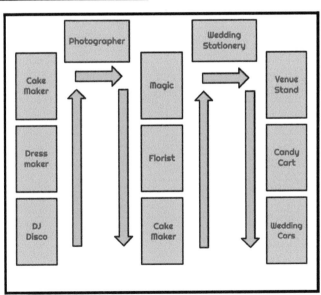

I do not want to be the first stand that they come to as most people will just pass it and move on, and the chance of them coming back is more remote, I would rather be in the middle so that when they have been round they will go back to the middle to attend the tables they either missed or want to visit again.

Wedding Fayre Costs.

The fees usually depend on the size of the fayre, generally a smaller fayre in the hotels and venues will normally be around £50 compared to upto around £200 - £250 for the bigger exhibition size shows.

The NEC is around £1200 for one of the smaller stands, one of my friends who booked there told me that once he had added electricity, set up, parking, hotels etc the whole event cost him around £3000.

The Stand.

A good wedding fayre stand should be a number of things. It should:

- Look professional.
- Be welcoming.
- Attract people to visit and view.
- Reflect your personality and the service you offer.
- A tool, not the main attraction.

Let's break these down and look at what they all mean.

Look professional.

Of course the stand should look professional, it should be uncluttered and neat. If you have give-a-ways or flyers etc they should be easily accessible as you do not want or need to be hunting for things whilst you are talking to potential customers.

Think about what you would want to see as you approach a stand and make your stand reflect this.

Be welcoming.

The stand should be a welcoming place, the attendees should feel comfortable coming over to have a look at what you offer.

I saw a stand with a huge sound system blaring out dance music and flashing lights, the stand was for a mobile casino and no one visited the stand all day.

Attract people to visit or view.

As well as being welcoming, you want to attract people to your stand, a clean, smart and attractive display will get interest and help bring people over to speak to you.

Reflect your personality and the service you offer.
Your stand is an extension of you, it should reflect who you are and what you are offering. I learnt a lot about this from looking at other peoples' stands. My good friend Juan (get used to this name, he will be mentioned a lot in this book), is an amazing wedding photographer and his stand is a perfect reflection of who he is and what he offers. He has big pictures in frames with beautiful images as well as smart photo books and amazing flyers and leaflets.

His stand reflects an elegant professional who takes care and pride in what he is offering, alongside this he is warm and welcoming and his stand is always full as is his diary.

Attendees will visit his stand, it looks great, it looks welcoming and Juan is charming and immensely likable.

A tool, not the main attraction.
The stand, once again, is an extension of you and your services, it is not the final product. The stand in reality is no more or less important than your flyers, business cards or other giveaways.

I learnt at a young age that you need the right tool for the job, so you need to make the stand the right tool.for what you are selling.

Let's have a look at a few stands and see how they compare and what makes them work.

I change my stand all the time, sometimes in big ways and sometimes in smaller more subtle ways.

For these examples I will share ideas and concepts from two wedding shows I regularly attend.

The first show is the Newmarket Wedding Show (NWS) which is held at a huge conference center at the Millennium Grandstand building at the Rowley Mile Racecourse. This fayre is huge with 4 stories and over 200 stands and generally attracts between 200 - 600 attendees.

The other show is at an amazing wedding venue called Swynford Manor (SM) just outside Newmarket. This is a smaller fayre with maybe 20 - 50 couples and around 20 stands.

At the NWS I have a six foot table provided by the event with a tablecloth. I push the table right to the back of my area and place two roller banners ON TOP of the table.

This will attract people from all around as these two banners are now visible from everywhere in the room.

Almost every show I will change the design of the roller banners, which is a small change but I do find it has a strong impact especially on returning attendees.

Here we have two images from the same venue. You can see how the banners are partially hidden in the first image and how much clearer they are in the second image.

In this image you can also see I have a small TV playing.

I created a video with all my advertising clips and promotional images that I thought looked great and created a looped video that would play for hours.

I remake this every show but this is one from 2018.

www.youtube.com/watch?v=w1gqPYX5I4Q

It plays without sound and just loops so I do not have to worry about restarting it at any point in the day.

Also on my table I have a couple of photo books of performance and reaction images and also a large number of postcards and business cards.

This allows attendees to approach the table and take a card themselves, which is very useful if I am in the middle of a performance or talking to someone else at the stand.

I will cover this side of the topic later in the chapter.

This is the wedding stand of a good friend and fellow magician John Morton, his personality and style is very sophisticated and his stand certainly reflects that.

He has a very minimalist approach and at the same time showcases his services perfectly.

I also love his use of easels to display the images he wants to show as well as the curtain backdrops which announces his performance aspect.

At the hotel venue, Swynford Manor, then I have a smaller, more appropriate set up.

One backdrop and no big table.

I use a couple of tall tables to hold my flyers etc and have a small performing table at the front with a small sign board on the floor.

Regardless of the fayre I never have a table out the front and chair etc behind.

I do not want to create a barrier between myself and the attendees.

Advertising on the day.
Now you have your space, your stand now you need to make sure that you have some amazing publicity material to share and give away to attendees on the day.

There are so many different options available to you for giveaways, I normally give away postcards or flyers and business cards as well as some cool stickers I made if any of the attendees had children with them.

Postcards.
Postcards are great, they are generally thicker than flyers and can display a great deal of information. With a good design they are pleasing to look at and will generally be kept longer than a normal flyer.

I have visited houses and seen my postcards clipped to message boards or on the fridge with a magnet holding it in place.

I also do have the same front design of my postcards made as fridge magnets and if I visit a home I will sling one up on the fridge door.

At the time of writing this is the front of my postcards.

We start with a nice quote, this is not over the top or too long and has pride of place at the very top.

Below that we have a great reaction shot, it is clear that something amazing is happening in the image and sets the tone for the front of the card.

Alongside the main there are three smaller images all displaying similar reaction shots.

Along the bottom of the card is the contact information displayed clearly and in bold fonts.

"We booked Wayne within minutes of meeting him, we loved his charm, humour and skill" - Claire & Dave
Contact Wayne now for a no-obligation consultation
www.waynegoodman.co.uk - wayne@waynegoodman.co.uk
call 07726 190078

The back of the card is similar to the front, but without one main image, instead we have 6 equal size images and a slightly longer quote.

Add to this the contact information again and the card is complete.

I am happy at present with this design and it seems to work well with the couples, as a contrast here are some of the older designs, some worked well and some not so much.

Wayne Goodman
Magician
www.waynegoodman.co.uk
07726 190078

Wayne Goodman is a unique
performer mixing Magic and
Comedy in his own style which
has taken him all over the world
from Las Vegas to Cancun,
Scandinavia to Spain.

Performing for many different
styles of audiences including
cruise ships and hotels, private
parties and business events
Wayne Goodman has the
experience and ability to make
your next event a SPECIAL
event.

Wayne Goodman
www.waynegoodman.co.uk

07726 190078 / wayne@waynegoodman.co.uk

Looking for a magician for your wedding?

Wayne Goodman is one of the most popular
wedding magicians working in the UK.

Wayne will entertain your guests with his
charming and friendly manner, then leave them
stunned and speechless with his amazing,
original and astounding magic.

www.waynegoodman.co.uk | wayne@waynegoodman.co.uk
Call or Text - 07726 190078

Wayne Goodman Entertainments

Wayne Goodman is a unique performer
mixing Magic and Comedy in his own style
which has taken him all over the world
from Las Vegas to Cancun, Scandinavia to
Spain.

Performing for many different styles of
audiences including cruise ships and
hotels, private parties and business events
Wayne Goodman has the experience and
ability to make your next event a SPECIAL
event.

Performing close up magic at a wedding or
trade show or performing on stage to
hundreds of people Wayne stands out from
other magicians due to his fun approach to
entertaining mixed with his amazing
sleight-of-hand

CALL NOW ...
to see how
Wayne can
make your
next event a
SPECIAL
event

www.waynegoodman.co.uk / 07726 190078

Now compare the back
design above with these
older designs.

These show too much text
that let's be honest will not be
read therefore it's a waste of
space.

The new design has lots of
colour, great images and just
the important text to get them
to either my website or to call
or email me.

I generally order these in bulk
from online printing
companies such as vistaprint
or instaprint and hand them
out to everyone at the fayre.

48

Flyers.
Personally I am not a fan of flyers, every other stand has flyers and they will be inundated with them and your flyer will get lost in the middle of them.

This is a flyer I used for a while. It looks great and got lots of great feedback on the day but did not garner a lot of enquiries compared to the postcards.

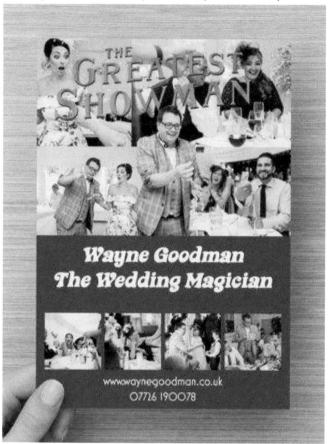

Banners.
Roller banners are great and affordable and can be changed as often as you like. I get between 5 and10 new banners every year for different reasons, they cost as little as £30 inc printing etc for the basic size and prices go up as the size increases.

Stickers.
Stickers are great giveaways for the kids, although I do have adults ask for them as well.

This is the design I use at the moment, one has a black ring and one a purple.

It also features the image of the purple and red hearts which enables me to do a simple but cool trick by forcing the 2 of hearts and then explaining there are two hearts on the sticker.

These are really simple in design but do have a strong impact on the families when they attend, I also use them at weddings or family shows too. Search online for the best deals. I generally order 1000 for around £30.

Business Cards.
Business cards are the lifeblood of my business, visit any shop or cafe in my home town and you will find my card attached to a board or available on the counter.

Over the years I have used many business cards from clear plastic cards to weird shaped cards, but I always come back to a normal business card size with a blank back.

I prefer the blank back as it allows me to use the cards in some of my effects and therefore gives me a legitimate reason to hand them out.

My current card looks like this.

Lots of colour and with the words going in different directions I get a lot of comments about how fun the card looks and is a good reflection of my personality.

The image in the top corner has an interesting backstory to it.

This is the original image:

When this was taken Apple were using their silhouette characters a lot and I decided to have a go at making my own, using this image.

It did not look good.

It looked like something you may see in a hostage video.

I decided it needed a little more character to it.

I added a small amount of colour to it, first just the card then I added the glasses and finally the collar.

This then became the background of the corner of the card.

Once again for comparison here are some of the older card designs, looking back now, I do wonder what was I thinking?

Wayne Goodman Entertainments
Comedy Magician

The No. 1 Choice for Magical Entertainment

Wayne Goodman

Office · 01638 560449
Mobile · 07726 190078
wayne@waynegoodman.co.uk

www.waynegoodman.co.uk

WAYNE GOODMAN
The Funeral Magician

Putting the
FUN
into
FUNERAL

www.waynegoodman.co.uk
wayne@waynegoodman.co.uk · 07726 190078

www.waynegoodman.co.uk
Phone: 01638 664401
Mobile: 07726 190078
wayne@waynegoodman.co.uk

WAYNE GOODMAN
"The Magician"

Close Up Magician
Comedy Cabaret
The Honest Cheat - Gambling Demonstration
The Magic Mind Reader

07726 190078
www.waynegoodman.co.uk
wayne@waynegoodman.co.uk

WAYNE GOODMAN

Wayne Goodman Entertainments
Comedy Magician / Close up Magic

The Wedding Fayre.
The saying goes, "You only get one 1 chance to make a first impression".

This is so important when you are meeting potential customers, especially for the first time.

You want to make sure you are maximising your potential and also, because of the outlay for the fayre you want to make a positive return on investment (ROI).

ROI.
Anytime you pay out for something, you should be looking to get the maximum back for what you have spent out on.

For example, if you pay £XX for an advert in a newspaper or on Facebook or Google etc then you should have an idea how much you will make from that advert.

If you pay £50 for a small wedding fayre and it only returns 3 enquiries then there was no real return on investment, however if you pay £50 for a small wedding fayre and you get to hand out 40 business cards and get 10 enquiries which you then convert into 8 wedding bookings (let's presume a wedding fee of £500 = 8 X 500 = £4000). This would be classed as a good return on the initial £50 investment.

Remember though that not all attendees will contact you on the day of the fayre, you may get an email in the few days or weeks following the fayre so it is important to find out where the customer met or saw you so you can keep track of the success or non-success of every fayre.

Making the most of the fayre.
The stand is set, the flyers are ready and the doors are about to be opened with all the attendees ready to come and start their wedding journey.
Here are a few ways you can maximise your presence for the day.

Social Media:
Love it or hate it, social media plays a huge part in our lives now and as such it is another tool to be utilised

I will post about the wedding fayre for weeks before the event so that everyone knows I will be attending. I have people come up to me at almost every fayre telling me they came along because they knew I would be there.

I also invite any new clients to come along so they can meet me in person, if needed, and also it guarantees that for certain times of the day I will have people on the stand.

I will also tag other wedding suppliers I know are at the same fayre, and if possible I will grab a picture with them at their stand and post and share online too, this not only promotes their services to my potential and actual clients but also promotes me to theirs.

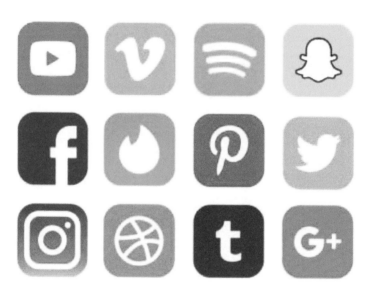

Data Collection.

The wedding fayre will hopefully be busy and you want to make sure that you do not lose or forget essential details about the potential clients you meet.

There are plenty of apps available for tablets that enable you to collect the required information and store it safely, I have an IPad set up ready in a stand but I also have a clipboard with approx 100 pre-printed sheets with the required questions which I ask the spectators to fill in and then place in a secure box on my stand.

Whatever way you choose to use, make sure they follow the up to date GDPR requirements. The GDPR legal requirements do tend to change over time so checking up on how you store and use information before the show is always best. You can find the current information on the government website.

Deposit Payment Idea.

If I have a client who is ready to pay their deposit, I will float the idea of combining the wedding fayre as a meeting place, they can swing by the fayre, check out any other items they are looking for, or if they are looking for some inspiration etc and at the same time, pop by my stand and we can sort the deposit.

This means some attendees will see a couple come up to pay their deposit at the fayre and nothing says you're in demand than consumers buying on the day.

I would also highly recommend a receipt book for the stand so that you can give a receipt to the client until you get home and can send a proper one, unless you use CRM software like the amazing Giggio in which case you can do the whole booking at the fayre in real time.

www.getgiggio.com/

Fun Items for your stand.
I have a few items on my stand that will generate a laugh for chuckle when people either view or visit my stand.

Facebook Frame:
One of my favourite items is a silly facebook frame, this is a frame that looks like it is a facebook post and is great for taking photos in.

These make great social media posts and I try to get pictures with both attendees and other wedding suppliers.

As you can see on this image the frame contains all my contact information.

This picture is on Juan and I at a wedding fayre.

Adult Creche:
The sign clearly states adult creche and advises leaving wayward and extra adults with me to watch and enjoy magic whilst they shop for other wedding essentials.

This sign is great and really shows off my sense of humour as well as showing I am fun and I love what I do.

It also creates an awesome talking point and is so visible around the room.

Attracting a crowd.
Having a busy stand is one step closer to having a hugely successful day. If you can consistently attract a large number of people to your stand you have already sold a large percentage of those watching on the idea of booking you as a magician.

Seeing a large number of people who are watching, gasping and laughing to your demonstration sells the fact that:

- You are entertaining.
- You are likable.
- You 100% know what you are doing.

The other people in the attendees group will also be raving about you and this will further raise your credibility with the decision maker.

Attracting a crowd is not as difficult as it sounds if you follow some simple rules and steps.

Be seen - Be booked.
Choose effects and routines that pack small and play big, this will maximise the visibility of the magic regardless of where people are watching from.

Encourage others to watch, or even better participate.
I will normally start by entertaining a small group and then encourage others who are looking over etc to come and watch as well.

Most of my effects I use allow for multiple selections of cards or choices etc so it is easy for me to get these new viewers to join in with what they are watching.

Less is more.
Keep the magic short and simple, you really want to avoid lengthy or complicated routines, you are not performing a full show just giving a demonstration of your skill and personality.

End on a high, but with a call to action.
Once you have a crowd, finish with a good routine that will get a big reaction.

Once the applause and laughter is dying down, call the crowd to action by TELLING them to collect a postcard or business card etc and then start bringing people in for the sales pitch.

If you have someone working on the stand with you, have them ready to start handing out flyers etc as soon as you end the routine.

On site assistance.
When I work the bigger shows I always try to have someone with me to work the stand alongside me.
For the last few years I have had the daughter of a friend of mine who would come along for the day and be on the stand with me.

Her job was just to hand out postcards all day and to ensure no one walked past the stand without taking a card, she would also chat to couples who were waiting to talk to me if I was dealing with another couple.

The Pitch.

The pitch is very important, it needs to be short but instructive, clear and concise, you should explain that you are an asset to the day and something they can not really afford to be without.

Make it short.

This is a pitch, it should be like a conversation and not a lecture, so stick to the important facts, you can fill in more information later if you get to the next stage of booking.

Clear and concise.

The pitch is a message, so stick to delivering it, no stories or going off on tangents.

Paint a picture.

Explain what the client's obstacles are going to be, and how you are going to solve those problems for them, or better still by having you, they can prevent those problems altogether.

Keep it light.

Try not to pound them down with too many facts or heavy information, give the key points and spark their interest.

DO NOT HARD SELL.

I have seen so many wedding fayre suppliers, magicians and not, who push and push and really hard sell the product. This is a mistake, I firmly believe that if anyone tries to hard sell anything to me, it is not worth having.

Nothing turns me off wanting something more than a hard seller. When I work at a wedding fayre stand, what I am selling is me, and if I do my job right, It should sell itself.

Fayre pricing.

One technique which can be very effective is a dedicated fayre pricing, this is a price for your services that is essentially "Today Only" price.

I generally run £50 off the quoted price if booked today type strategy.

Package deals.

Everyone likes a bargain and rather than decreasing your price, a much better business model is to offer more service for an increase in the price.

A lot of magicians I have seen have attractive package deals with catchy names like Silver - Gold - Platinum, and most follow a similar pattern.

The Silver package will be the most basic.

The Gold package will offer more services and have a sharp increase in price.

The Platinum package will offer even more services but the price will not be much more than the gold package. (This is for example purposes).

Silver	Gold	Platinum
Basic price eg £300	Medium price eg £750	High Price eg £800
1 hour close up	3 hours close up	3 hours close up
Close up magic	Close up magic	Close up magic
xxx	Special performance for Bride and Groom	Special performance for Bride and Groom
xxx	xxx	30 Cabaret Show after meal
xxx	xxx	1 hour close up magic for evening guest

The silver package delivers the basic service

The gold package will initially be their first choice as it delivers a good amount of time with a nice selection of services included in the package.

When they see the platinum package is only £50 more and they get a whole a whole lot more for their money, this will be the most popular option.

How you structure your own packages is of course up to you, my packages are different to the example given above and I tend to change it every few years to allow for different add ons and extras I am using.

Offer a free consultation.
Any B&G I speak to will be offered a free - no obligation - consultation that they can arrange at a time and place that suits their requirements.

This gives me more time to speak, demonstrate and sell the services I have available. It also allows me to offer a more personalised service that is more suited to their bespoke day and makes them feel like they are getting something of value by having special access to your time and expertise.

Know the problems before they do.
When you speak to the B&G, show that you know your business, and you understand the problems they will face, you have encountered them before and you can deal with them as required.

A good example of this is this.

"The B&G will have the misconception that during the B&G's photo session everyone will rejoice in conversation and reminisce on the amazing celebration of unity they have had the privilege of witnessing"

This is not the case, in reality whilst the B&G are off having pictures taken the rest of the party will stand in small groups, not interacting with anyone outside their own small group. They will be drinking and counting down the minutes until either they can get another drink or they will be called through to eat.

So now we know the problem, how do we fix it?

Simple, book me to keep everyone entertained, break the ice between groups and build the atmosphere.

When I chat to the B&G I will convey this in a manner that addresses that I know what I am doing and I can be trusted to deliver on this expertise.

Your guests will be entertained with the perfect mixture of sleight of hand, comedy and astounding magic. Don't worry though, I will make sure you get to see the best magic, and will make time to see you during the reception.

Building the right atmosphere during the reception is key to having the perfect day, my magic is the best way to break the ice and get everyone talking so when they go to their tables, they are actively discussing what they have just seen.

Once everyone is seated (including yourselves) I will move around the room creating a fun atmosphere that will keep your guests entertained between courses and more importantly break the ice at the tables. Every couple worries about the seating plan, and trying to get people to sit with others they know, but after I have left the table, every guest at the table will be animated and actively chatting about what has just happened.

Leading us into the evening where I can wander around and interact with guests so that the atmosphere is maintained and enhanced into the night.

Write down and rehearse what you want to say, anticipate the questions you will get and have the answers ready. Know your job, your audience and your customers so when they have a concern or a question, you are already in a position to answer it and relieve any concerns they may have.

To end this marathon of a chapter I am going to wish you good luck with your fayres and above everything else, enjoy them and have a good time.

Wedding Advertising

Another area for marketing yourself is through specialist forums such as websites and social media groups and magazines.

There is a lot of discussion and debate about the best place to advertise or at least the best place to get your website or advertisement mentioned.

Being part of an article or even better writing your own article for a wedding magazine or website is a great way to get your name or business in the public eye to a large number of people who may be in the market to booking your service.

There are far too many magazines and forums to post a list here, plus as with all things like this, by the time this is printed, read etc the list would have changed drastically with some gone forever and a whole bunch of new ones available to find.

Instead I thought I would share with you an experience I went through to test whether or not these types of advertising work or not.

**** Disclaimer ****

These experiences are mine and mine alone and should not reflect the experience of all service providers etc.

Magazines.
I have spent thousands over the years advertising in wedding magazines and local directory magazines as well as back in the day, putting an advert in the Yellow Pages.

I have tried small ads, medium ads and even half and full page ads, and I can say with all honesty, I found almost all of them a waste of time.

I even paid to have my business card included with a wedding magazine that would be handed out to thousands of couples at the national wedding show, this cost me £90 and the only call I got was from another wedding fayre asking if I wanted to do the same for their fayre, I kindly declined.

I truly believe that print advertising is a waste of time and money, most couples will take a magazine if handed one, but I seriously doubt they will even open it let alone read it.

It's a nice idea but with the advent of the internet and google it has, in my honest opinion, become redundant and outdated.

However, this does not mean it will not work for you.

If you are going to advertise in any kind of magazine, you need to do some homework and make sure it is the right magazine for you and your business.

Do some research, if a magazine or website contacts you, ask them for a sample copy of the magazine, or a link to the website.
Once you have this information you can get to work.

If it is a magazine you can read the content, check the layout and see how diverse and well placed the adverts are.

If it is a website you can check the dates of the posts and see how up to date they keep the content.

The best part is with both formats you can see the other advertisers and this means you can contact them and ask how the adverts are doing for them, if they are getting leads and are quality leads or not.

At the end of the day the publishers do not care about you or your business and will sell you the hype, they will sell you the dream or in some cases the lie, that a small advert on their content (magazine or website) will reap you all the gold at the end of the rainbow, when in reality they do not care and just want to sell the column inches.

Adwords.

Google is revered as the best place, at least online, to advertise, but with the best comes the best price, so be prepared to spend, spend and spend before you see any results.

Adwords essentially targets keywords people type in and then promotes you to those searches.

So for weddings you would want to select a bunch of keywords that will be the search for weddings.

The main problem is the cost of the individual keywords, which does not guarantee you being seen by the right people, and with anything of this nature it will be distinctly hit and miss, with the misses being a much bigger part of the equation.

Social Media advertising.

I have met many people who make a living telling others how to use social media advertising, and yet almost all of these "experts" fall at the first hurdle when I question them on specific needs and requirements.

Their pitches are great to a group of people who know nothing, but if you have any idea about what you need or require you are better off spending a few hours and trying to work it out for yourself.

Over the last 12 years I have spent a few thousand pounds on advertising on facebook and although I got a lot of impressions, they did not lead anywhere and so I ended up closing all the ads down.

Now this is not to say you should not use social media to advertise your business, but there are better and easier ways to do it without spending thousands of pounds.

Join wedding groups that are not just full of suppliers but aimed at couples who are looking or open to recommendations.

I am also a member of groups that are run by wedding venues etc, these groups tend to tag me A LOT when couples mention entertainment.

These social media groups have saved me a lot of money and have reaped me a huge number of leads that have been converted to booking.

Write a wedding blog.
This is a brilliant way to get your name out there and shared a lot.
Write a weekly blog and share it across all your social media platforms and send out via email.

Choose subjects that not only highlight your business but also showcase other suppliers too. I posted a blog post about my friends who own a wedding cake business and this got a lot of attention and shared a lot.

This led to the readers checking out other posts I had written and thus they found out about my business and led to quality leads.

Wedding Directory.
The wedding directory is not a bad way to get your name into the game but remember you have purchased a small spot in a much larger picture.

Your advert may be near the top for a while but it will soon drift down the list and be lost in the forest of other suppliers.

My advice for this is, use it while it works then reconsider other methods to be seen.

Website

This chapter has proven to be a nightmare to write, and has actually been rewritten almost a dozen times, mainly because trying to describe the perfect website is almost impossible.

Speaking with other wedding professionals showed that everyone has their own opinions, they have their own ideas and they all know what will and what will not work for their own website.

Instead I will give a brief overview of my own site, and tell you what works for me, and what has not worked over the years.

Post information not your ego.
Your website is a window into who you are and what you are selling, so make sure it is not showing you in a bad light.

It is very easy, when writing content for a website to lose yourself in your own ego and you end up writing something so outlandish and exaggerated that no one will look at you twice.

Instead write from the heart and make a website about the person looking.

The easiest way to do this is to think of the reasons why they are on the website and then write content that will,

- Answer any questions they may have.
- Suggest ideas they may not have considered.
- Show your personality.

It is not hard to construct positive content about weddings, kids shows or parties, these are positive occasions so make your content about what you do, how you do it and why you are the best choice for it.

The easiest way to do this is to never write in the first person, this way it does not sound like you are over confident or arrogant.

Which sounds better?

"I am an amazing magician, I am an expert in close up magic and I am hilarious, so book me now and you are guaranteed a brilliant time with me making everyone laugh and doing my amazing magic".

Or

"Wayne Goodman is not only an amazing magician but a true expert when it comes to working close up doing magic, add to that his comedic timing and endless stream of jokes and you and your guests will love the magic of Wayne Goodman".

The first one is all, me, me, me, whilst the second one is informative and has the narrative of being told as a recommendation, not as someone stroking their own ego.

Pictures.
The saying goes, a picture is worth a thousand words, so good quality pictures of people enjoying what you do is invaluable.

Make friends with the wedding photographer, if you are not already, and suggest they stand behind you for a few of the tricks so they can catch the amazing faces you will create for them.

I will also do a few tricks for them during the day when they are not super busy, then towards the end of the day ask if you can have any of the photos they have taken of you or the amazed guests, I normally find this is not an issue as I give them my business card and a folded in half £20 note.

This friendly approach will normally get you some amazing pictures for your website and promo material.

If you ask, after the day, if you can buy the images then they will probably offer you as many pics as you want for £10 - £50 per image, much better to sweet talk them at the wedding and chance a £20 for a whole bundle.

If you do use the photos on the website make sure you add a credit to the photographers too, this is always appreciated as you are promoting their services.

Great reaction shots are invaluable to your website.

Less is more.
This is one lesson I learnt years ago, and something that I refer to in almost everything I do.

Less is more seems like a contradiction but the idiomatic and proverbial expression "less is more" means that simple is sometimes better or more effective than elaborate.

You do not need 500 pictures of people at weddings if you have 5 really great pictures.

You do not need pages upon pages of text not really saying anything when carefully chosen text with direct and to the point information will have a bigger impact with the client.

Make your website full of information but uncluttered, bright but not overpowering and most importantly portray you in a good but honest way that promotes the service you are providing.

Another great way to get photos is to, with permission, bring along someone capable of taking some pictures and getting them to follow you around getting some pictures of you and the guests etc.

I will, of course, speak to the bride and groom before the day and ask if they have any objections to this, and that I will happily share with them all the photos I get from the day.

For the bride and groom this is a great addition set of free pictures, that will be entirely made up of their guests having a wonderful time.

The last way, and this can either be brilliant or a complete waste of time, is to bring your own camera, a cheap digital camera with decent spec can be bought for around £50, and give it to a older child at the wedding and ask them to snap some pictures of you with some of the groups.

I will normally approach the family and do some magic and then ask the child if they fancy helping out for a while, and seeing more amazing magic.

I have never had a child turn me down for this, and I will normally give them £5 or £10 at the end when we are done for their efforts.

These pictures will become one of the three B's

Brilliant - Blurry - Bonkers

Brilliant.
Sometimes you will get some photos that look amazing, they really capture the moment and the money is well spent.

To be honest if you only get a couple of decent pictures or even just one then it is worth it.

This was taken at a wedding I was working at by a 13 yr old boy who I gave the camera to. It is a great shot that captures the moment perfectly.

Blurry.
A lot of the time you will end up with a lot of pictures that are blurry or out of focus, but this is the risk, you have a child with a camera not a professional expert photographer.

Bonkers.
These are the pictures that you scratch your head about and wonder why they were even taken in the first place.

I once looked through the photos at the end of the night and saw pictures of leaves, pictures of an upturned glass on a table and even a picture of a broken plate.

Obviously this was some child genius who probably will end up taking photos that are sold for millions and have gallery showings around the globe, brilliant but not what I was hoping for, they still made me smile.

I will also ask anyone snapping pictures on their phone if they would be happy to share them, this is another way that almost always works.

The last tip on photo's is to ask the B&G to share any pictures they get from the day, either from the professional photographer or from friends and family who send them, this will normally elicit a good selection of images you can use.

Normally a B&G will have a social media page on sites like facebook and this is a goldmine for shared photos and messages about how good the magician was.

Videos.
Videos on a website are also so important, and a great opportunity to really showcase your personality.

Videography has become much more popular over the last few years and people now have amazing Cameras on their phones so do not be afraid to ask someone to share the video if you see them recording, this again can lead to some amazing footage that you can edit and use on your site etc.

FAQ.

A FAQ, (Frequently Asked Question) page on your website is essential, it has a number of benefits, not only for your business and service but also for your website too.

It allows an opportunity to improve your SEO, (Search Engine Optimisation), through targeted content development. Targeted Content is content that is designed for a niche market audience, essentially its content that is aimed at a specific audience.

FAQs also allow the clients to see that you know your business, you have been asked these questions many times and you are prepared for them. This is a reassuring moment that will allow them to be more relaxed and more open to asking questions.

It also allows the clients to get past these regular initial questions and when you meet for a consultation or a phone call, you are already 2 steps forward than you would be if you did not have these FAQs posted.

Blog.

Hosting And writing a blog is a brilliant way to connect with your clients and potential clients on a regular basis.

I will mention blogs in other chapters but having a blog on your website enables you to place yourself in the industry as an entertainment expert.

someone who blogs about themselves and other suppliers services which will be read and referred to by B&Gs, whilst at the same time, driving traffic to your website has to be the most prominent example of a win-win.

Easy and clear user friendly navigation.

A website that is easy to navigate with clear menu options etc will be more attractive to a potential client than one that is a maze of options.

Keeping it simple with clear headings and subsections will keep the clients interest whilst at the same time being informative and useful to your business.

Testimonials.
Almost every industry now has a website dedicated to reviews etc,

- Trip advisor.
- Trust a trader.
- Yelp.
- Angies List.
- Facebook reviews.

Some are dedicated to a specific industry whilst others have review subsections so people can search and industry and leave or read relevant reviews.

So why not put up some reviews you have received either in emails, letters, cards or online.

DO NOT make these up, only use real testimonials as you will soon be caught out and your reputation ruined if they are found to be fake.
There was a magician in mid 2010's who had a page on their website full of images of them with celebrities, these turned out to be terrible wax models and not the good ones like you get at Madame Tussauds.

Optimised for any device.
Most website buildsite will allow you to see your website as it will be viewed on a computer or on a mobile device.

USE THIS FEATURE, and make sure your website looks good on both, otherwise you will lose potential customers who check you on their mobile or tablet before getting to see you on the computer, if they bother with a computer at all.
Call to action.

A call to action, (CTA), is a marketing term that refers to an instruction that will lead to an action.

A good example of this is:

Book Wayne Goodman Now

Nice and clear, and you do not need any guidance on why you are clicking it.

One of my favorite CTAs is Learn More.

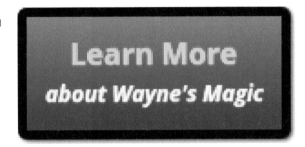

This will be used on a webpage or digital advertising that will encourage the potential client to click through and be taken to a dedicated service page.

Do not confuse CTA with Clickbait, and avoid clickbait at all costs.

Clickbait is a text or a thumbnail link that is designed to attract attention and to entice users to follow that link and read, view, or listen to the linked piece of online content, with a defining characteristic of being deceptive.

Dedicated service pages.
A dedicated service page means a webpage that is dedicated to a specific service you offer.

For instance if, like me, you do multiple shows, you can now dedicate a page to each of these shows.

Weddings, close up, Parties, events, trade shows, lectures and the list goes on and on and on.

Some people prefer to brand themselves and have dedicated websites for each of the shows, keeping wedding and kids shows apart, again this is a personal choice and will depend on how you want to market your business.

Contact Page.

If you want to be booked, then you need to be contactable. Lots of people will just have a contact page with a form to fill out and no actual contact information.

I do not like this, although almost all my clients will contact me via email, I like to give them the option of calling me also.

This is however, down to personal choice.

My website has a very easy to follow contact page that is clear and to the point.

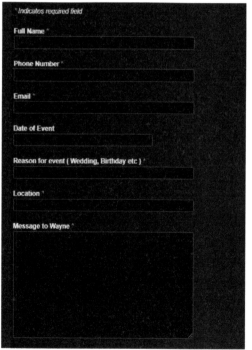

Name, contact details and some relevant information.

The contact page should not be a huge distraction full of pictures etc but rather less is more.

A simple contact form that links to your website or some text telling them how to contact you.

I also have a small section beneath this that allows the potential client to inform me which show they would like.

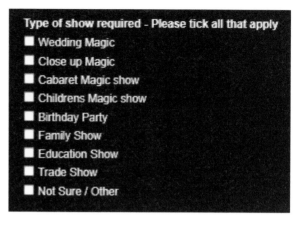

Type of show required - Please tick all that apply
- Wedding Magic
- Close up Magic
- Cabaret Magic show
- Childrens Magic show
- Birthday Party
- Family Show
- Education Show
- Trade Show
- Not Sure / Other

Fresh and quality content, updated regularly.
Keeping your website up to date with fresh content is essential if you want it to work well with Google and other search engines.

These search websites will look at your website and if they see that it has not changed since the last time it scanned it, then they will presume, rightly or wrongly, that the site is not in use or has become outdated or even obsolete.

If they view the website and see new content, new images, video or a new blog post etc they will be more likely to share the site on searches as it is obviously a modern up to date, well maintained site that the users will want to view and use.

Hire an expert or do it yourself.
Building a website has never been easier, there are loads of options from wordpress to wix for people who want to have a go at building their own site.

There are some options for building your own website using just coding, but if you are not familiar with how this works, I would recommend looking at other options.

Some websites like Wix or Weebly allow an easy to use web building platform which is essentially a drag and drop web builder. You can place text, pictures and videos where you want them as well as building in essential plugins like contact forms, youtube links and photo slideshows.

A good friend of mine, Andy Chase, also pointed me at Google sites, which is a free to use, very simple drag and drop website builder. I have spent a few hours there today and was amazed at how easy it is to build a site and it does give you a lot more freedom than some of the self build sites.

If you are feeling a little more adventurous, Wordpress is an exceptional website builder, it is not the easiest builder but once you get used to it you can build some amazing sites.

The other way to build a website is to hire a professional web builder.
Like any service industry you will find many levels of expertise and an equal number of levels of price.

Do a search and find a builder who reflects the kind of website you are looking for.

If you want to check out an amazing website designer then take a look at,

www.monster-creations.com

Here are my top 10 must haves for your website.
- Easy and clear user friendly navigation.
- Good design and layout.
- Fresh and quality content, updated regularly.
- Clear Call to action.
- Blog.
- Testimonials.
- FAQs.
- Contact Information.
- Dedicated service pages.
- Optimised for any device.

And 4 things you want to avoid.
- Music.
- Auto-Playing videos.
- Flash.
- Clickbait.

Wedding suppliers

When I started working at weddings etc I noticed that I was constantly working around the same people, the same cake makers, the same photographers etc etc etc.

These people quickly became my friends and when we meet up at wedding fayres it has a real positive impact on the day.

To this day I am part of a group of suppliers who meet regularly for drinks or food and we all refer to each other as a wedding supplier family.

When I first worked with Juan, the wedding photographer, he told me I should definitely attend the Newmarket Wedding Show and even put in a recommendation to the organiser.

It was at this fair I met Rachel and Graham who run an amazing wedding cake business, Julie who specialises in wedding stationery and Lucie who deals with wedding decorations and seat covers.

I had met all these people at weddings leading up to the fayre and it was great to see them all in one place, they quickly accepted me into their wedding circle and by the end of the day they had all sent multiple couples to my stand and recommended me.

Wedding suppliers should become an extension of your own business, they will recommend you and you should reciprocate this and do the same for them.

I have a wedding recommendations page on my website:

www.waynegoodman.co.uk/waynes-wedding-recommendations

Each logo on this page is actually a link to their website, so I am able to share this with clients and recommend all my favorite suppliers.

The only prerequisites I have for this page is that I have worked with the supplier and I highly rate them and their service.

So why is it important to get to know other wedding suppliers?

Well apart from the recommendations aspect already mentioned, here are some hints and tips about creating a bond with other suppliers.

Join a networking group.
There are plenty of groups all over social media that enable you to chat and discuss weddings with other suppliers, but do not forget to look closer to your own home. I am part of a couple of small business networking groups in my hometown that not only cater for any businesses but have a lot of the same wedding suppliers I know as members.

They are not the competition.
I know a lot of professionals who see everyone else as competition, not only people in their own profession but across the whole industry.
I work closely with a number of wedding magicians and will wholeheartedly recommend them when I am not available for a wedding.

Work WITH and not AGAINST the other companies and if you share, like and promote them in a positive way, it will make you shine too.

Become an expert in your chosen field.

Whenever my friends are talking about weddings and entertainment is mentioned, my name is mentioned. My friends and fellow wedding suppliers know that I KNOW my business and what is required for almost every event, not just weddings.

I have shown through helping them with clients, being seen at events and weddings etc that not only do I know what I am doing but also I know what I am talking about and I know my industry.

Building supplier contacts should be your main aim.

There is only one real constant in weddings, and that is the suppliers.

Every month, every year you will meet new leads that once qualified will lead to bookings etc but once the event has happened, a lot of these clients will vanish, of course some will keep in touch and there is always a potential, especially with magicians and entertainers, for future work but for most suppliers it is a one hit gig, after all who plans on using a wedding cake maker again.

Building up a database or network of wedding suppliers and creating your dream suppliers group or as we have it, our wedding suppliers family means you can expand your service recommendation list, grow your business and flourish amongst other like minded professionals.

I have earned thousands over the years, from recommendations, referrals and support from my supplier friends, and for the most part all it has cost me is a few cups of coffee, a few social meet ups and a little bit of my time to recommend them.

But remember when you create a symbiotic relationship, they need your help as much as you need their help.

Common problems.
It is easy to believe that the problems you face are yours and yours alone, however nothing is further from the truth. Speaking with other suppliers showed me that they had faced similar problems or issues and told me how they had dealt with them.

One problem I was encountering was that my website blog posts were not getting good "seen" or "read" numbers and I was unsure about what I could do that would mean that when I share the blog post it would be seen by more people.

My friend Jason, who is a whizz at IT stuff, told me NOT to share the url of the blog in the actual post, rather share it in the comments section.

Most Social Media sites do not want to share posts that take people away from the host site, but have no issues with the comments section.

This meant that by sharing a post and then advising the link is in the comments I was able to get a broader reach and an increase in likes and shares.

Here is an example of the difference from a post experiment I did in 2020 for a magic lecture I was giving.

The first post was put up at 2pm on the first day and the second post was put up at 2pm on the following day.

Wayne Goodman
July 11th 2020 at 2pm

Getting married or know someone who is?

Check out my new blog post about an amazing wedding supplier I work with a lot.

www.waynegoodman.co.uk/blog/elegant-and-beautiful

Pls like and share so everyone can check it out.

Like · Comment · Share

66 people like this.

47 shares

Write a comment...

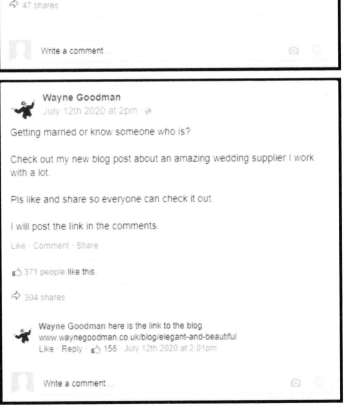

Wayne Goodman
July 12th 2020 at 2pm

Getting married or know someone who is?

Check out my new blog post about an amazing wedding supplier I work with a lot.

Pls like and share so everyone can check it out.

I will post the link in the comments.

Like · Comment · Share

371 people like this.

304 shares

Wayne Goodman here is the link to the blog
www.waynegoodman.co.uk/blog/elegant-and-beautiful
Like · Reply · 156 · July 12th 2020 at 2.01pm

Write a comment...

As you can see the difference speaks for itself, the first post hit a small number of likes and shares whilst the second post hit a much bigger audience and subsequently got more likes and shares.

This little nugget of information has meant I have been able to get more people to my blog, which has meant more people to my website and an increase in enquiries and bookings.

This is one example of sharing a problem or concern or in this case a frustration with my wedding fayre family and having not only a constructive and positive response but somethat that enabled me to radically change my approach to sharing important information.

Professional friendships and friends who are professionals.
As mentioned before you will hear the name Juan a lot in this book, Juan is an amazing wedding photographer.

I recommend him at least 5 times a week to clients for all kinds of events and I am someone he has taken to clients which has led to so many weddings and parties and even a trip down the Thames on a business cruise.

Juan has a young daughter who is 15 months older than my own daughter.

These two are thick as thieves and love social meet ups and chatting about tik tok and who is the biggest influencer on youtube etc.

I have got to know Juan and his wife and family on a personal level and he has been an amazing support to what I have achieved and what I am continuing to strive towards.

Do not underestimate how much of an impact having professional friends can have when it comes to working, not only does it take away a lot of the stress when you do have a problem etc but it also makes some of the more mundane times (like a slow day at a wedding fayre when no one turns up) seem a lot more fun.

I have worked with some amazing suppliers including photographers, cake makers, boutiques, Djs, discos, bands, videographers, toastmasters, shadow cutters (see below), makeup, Hairdressers, Travel companies, musicians, harpists, saxophone players, phone booths, decorations, candy carts, venues, drones, BBqs, Chefs, Hog roasts, mobile bars, cars, dancers, singing waiters ... the list could go on forever.

This is an amazing silhouette of my profile made by an amazing cutter Mark Conlin, his website is amazing too.

www.theshadowcutter.co.uk/

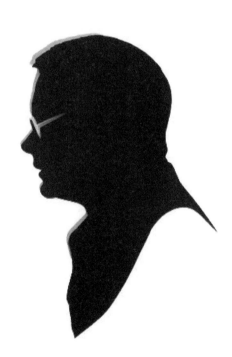

To end this chapter here are a couple of gifts I have given and received from my wedding supplier family group.

From my friend Juan.
He brought me a fanta Jack Daniels decanter.
I got him a photographer's mug.

My friend Julie likes to think outside the box a little and got us all a beautiful little box that says

"If you feel there is something missing in your life, it is almost always a biscuit"

It did contain some biscuits too.

Wedding Venues

Wedding venues are, as mentioned in the previous chapter on wedding fayres, part of the big three.

Not only are they an essential part of any wedding day, the most expensive part of the wedding day but they also dictate how and where you will be working.

I have had the pleasure and honour of working in some of the most beautiful venues around the world including a mountainside resort about an hour from Alicante in Spain, a cruise ship in the Baltic and a Steam Train along the north coast of Norfolk.

Every venue is different, but take the time to learn the names of the staff, from the reception to the kitchen, the bar staff and waiting staff and of course the wedding team and the management.

I am on the recommendation list for all the main wedding venues within 30 miles of my home, this has happened mainly because I take the time to make sure everyone at the venue knows who I am, including going into the kitchens before I go home and doing a couple of tricks for the unseen and unsung heroes of the day.

This has also led me to being booked for Christmas parties and other special events at the venues including the venue's own staff parties and award nights.

Arriving at the venue.
When you arrive at the venue make sure you park in the right place and make your way inside.

If you are booked for the day time then you will find that the wedding staff will be very busy.

If there is no one in the reception area the best place to head to, so that you are not in the way, is to the bar area, normally the bar staff will be able to help you to where you need to be.

If you are arriving for the evening party then the bar will be the last place to seek help, as they will probably be inundated with both day and night guests. Most of the time you will be able to find a member of the wedding team as they will be more relaxed after the wedding breakfast.

Setting up.
I will normally have my close up stuff set ready to go but if you need to get prepped before you can start then ask the venue staff if there is a side room or a small space you can use to sort yourself.

Do this in a polite manner and not a demand, I know this sounds like common sense but I have seen supposed professionals acting like spoilt brats because the venue staff (which has nothing to do with the booking) can't or won't

A place for your bags.
Unless I am booked for a cabaret spot or a children's magic spot, I only have my close up bag.

If I am booked for extra shows (stand up, kids etc), then I will speak to the venue before the day and arrange a better parking space and I will know where I need to store my cases until I need to set up etc.

The staff will be too busy with everything else to deal with me on the day so a five minute call beforehand is essential.

When I arrive I now know where to go and also they know I am coming and it is not a surprise to find me on the doorstep with cases and sound equipment etc.

If I am just booked for the close up then I will only have a small bag with me that I can easily find a safe place to store it while I am working.

Most of the time I can leave it behind a display or table or even in reception.

My close up case is small and black and does not look like it contains anything of interest or value.

The bag contains everything I need for the day and keeps it organised and neat.

Learn the lay of the land.
If you have never been to the venue before, a quick look at the website will tell you almost everything you will need to know about the venue and the layout of the rooms etc.

I will, however, normally arrive in plenty of time so that I can have a quick look around and make sure I am familiar with the set up.

I have a quote that perfectly sums up being prepared and doing your research before you arrive,

> *"By failing to prepare, you are preparing to fail"*

Do your research, know the facts and arrive prepared.

The Booking

The Booking.
Taking a booking does not have to be a scary or intimidating thing, and yet when I speak to magicians a lot of them say they hate the booking process because they are scared they have missed out information, or not asked the right questions.

Regardless of when you speak to the B&G, you need to be prepared to ask the pertinent questions that will give you the information that you need to be able to confirm a booking.

A lot of people will ask, "How much does it cost?".

Whilst it seems that this is quite a simple question, the answer may not be so easy to answer without some basic information first.

Imagine that a couple approach you and say,
"How much?"

you say "£450"

They are over the moon and say they want to book you, then they announce the wedding is 4 hours drive from your house, they want you for the daytime and the evening and they also want a kids show for the speeches.

Before you ever answer a question about cost, you need to know you have all the facts and important information so you can quote an appropriate fee.

So what information is needed before you can talk about confirming a booking?
I was once told that a booking is based on what a client wants.

Whilst this is true, it is not completely true, as most clients do not know what they want.

They want a magician for their wedding, that is about as far as it goes in their minds, but for you as the supplier you need to tell them what they actually want from you.

I have a number of questions that I need answering before I can take a booking.

- What date is the wedding?
- Where is the wedding taking place?
- Is the wedding taking place at the same place as the reception?
- What time are the couple getting married?
- How many guests are they inviting to the day and evening reception?

I ask all these questions as part of a conversation as I have seen other suppliers at wedding fayres etc almost interrogate the B&G, by engaging in a friendly conversation about their upcoming wedding I can get all the information that I need.

So why do these questions matter?

By having all the correct information I can advise on the best options for the B&G.

What date is the wedding?
Obviously I need to check and make sure I am available.

Where is the wedding taking place?
This let's me plan the day incase of other shows etc as well as taking into account travelling costs.

Is the wedding taking place at the same place as the reception?
This is very important, if the wedding is at the reception venue then I want to be ready as soon as the ceremony ends.

If however, the ceremony is at a church or other venue then I need to know the estimated time of arrival at the venue so I can arrive at the appropriate time.

What time are the couple getting married?

Most wedding ceremonies take between 30 - 45 minutes depending on the way the ceremony is conducted and how much the registrar loves the sound of their own voice.

I can advise on my start time based on how long the ceremony should take.

How many guests are they inviting to the day and evening reception?
Most people will have between 25 - 90 guests for the day time ceremony, and between 30 - 70 more for the evening party, however every B&G will have an idea of how their day will be and who they want to invite.

I have done a wedding with 12 guests and another with over 350.

If they are looking at more than 150 guests I will always recommend a second magician to work alongside me.

Consultation.
I will always recommend a no obligation consultation either face to face or over zoom etc.

This is a great opportunity to really have a good chat with the couple and for them to see I am more than someone who is just trying to get their money.

My consultations always include a few jokes and a couple of carefully chosen tricks, but when it comes to speaking to the B&G, even though I almost always know what they will say and what questions they will ask, I always LISTEN and RESPOND ACCORDINGLY, instead of passively listening and then just carrying on with some prepared dialogue.

The consultation normally takes place after a commitment to book, however if they have been recommended to me and do not know anything about who I am or what I do, other than what they have been told and/or seen on my website then I have this one opportunity to sell them the package and make them realise they not only want me, they need me for their wedding day.

ROI.

Most people know ROI stands for return on investment, and for B&G this means making sure, if they book you, they are getting a ROI or value for money.

If they spend £500 on a magician and all he does is chat up the bridesmaids, ignore large groups of the party and only works for 30 minutes when he is booked for 2 hours then that is pretty poor service and not a good return on their investment.

If they are thinking of booking you then the first thing you need to do is make sure they see that you know what you are doing and you are value for money.

A good place to do this is to place yourself as PART of their big day and not just an accessory. If you share advice and make suggestions all of a sudden your worth and value have increased.

Do you want to be some extra with a deck of cards?

Or

Do you want to be a valuable asset that has not only been an amazing part of their amazing day, but you are an essential part of the planning process which pointed out suggestions or made recommendations that were instrumental in making the whole day a success.

I know which one I would rather be.

Planning the day.

When I am discussing my part of their wedding day I want to show how much I actually bring to the day, and what I can potentially add to their day too.

I want to show the B&G that I know what I am doing, I can accommodate their requirements and at the same time calm any nerves about their day and let them know that they can relax and enjoy their day and leave the work to the people they are trusting to do it.

If I have worked at the venue a lot, I will be sure to let them know this, as it shows I will know the inner workings of the venue.

For instance, one sentence I use a lot when I am speaking to the bride and groom is this.

"So you're getting married at "Insert Venue Name Here", That is a beautiful venue, and I know the staff there, they have an amazing team who really know their stuff."

So from this one sentence I get to place myself as part of the team, I know the staff, they are amazing and the venue is beautiful.

It does not sound like much when you just say it, when I say it to the B&G it resonates with their planning, confirms that someone else loves the venue and reassures them that the staff will be amazing.

Seating Plan.
Most couples will really fret when it comes to the seating plan, in fact when I speak to couples, they confess that the seating plan keeps them up at night and they have to write and rewrite it multiple times.

I use this information when I am speaking to them.

"The biggest issue you will have is the seating plan, you will end up with a table we call the oddbins table. This table will have, for example, your cousin and his work friend who have no connection".

"They will eat and barely talk, and after the meal, they will say how beautiful the bride is, thank you both for the invite and then head off home".

At this point the B&G will be nodding and agreeing with me,

"However, when I am working at a wedding I will make sure that it doesn't matter who is sitting at what table, everyone will be engaged and animated and discussing what I have just done when I leave the table".

This is again a confident statement, and as I am speaking with authority and knowledge of experience it will have the impact and make the impression that I want to.

It also allows me to show that, as well as being a great ice breaker and amazing addition to the atmosphere, it is also solving a problem that they may be encountering.

When I listen to the running of the day and gently insert my presence into each section it enables me to show them exactly what I bring to the event.

This will then have the knock on effect of them seeing me as a working part of the machine and a cog they can't afford to be without.

Remember though you need to talk with authority but not be arrogant, do not push too hard either, a gentle nudge and a suggestion on how you have helped in the past is enough, too much and you will jeopardise the booking.

In the words of Will Smith in the film "Hitch",

"It is no longer your job to make her like you".
"it is your job, NOT TO MESS IT UP".

You have the booking, do not ruin it now by being too pushy.

Package options.
As mentioned in the chapter on wedding fayres, some suppliers and some magicians will offer a package deal.

This can be great for the B&G, who may be working within a budget and will appreciate the different options.

Fee's.
This is a hot topic, and one subject that is guaranteed to cause many arguments on magic forums and in magic chats.

The truth is, it is your business and so therefore it is only your business how much you charge, but that does not mean you should not think very carefully about how much you are charging and you want to make sure you are not overcharging or undercharging.

Too high a fee and you will outprice yourself from the event, too low and you will scare the client away, think of it like this.

You want a new kitchen and you approach 10 local builders for a quote

1 builder submits a quote of £40,000 for the kitchen you want.

The 2nd builder submits a quote of £1,250.

8 of the builders submit quotes ranging from £10,000 - £15,000.

Builder 1 has submitted a quote that is massively above any other quote, this could be due to better materials, a more expensive design etc but it does place the quote way above the others.

Builder 2 has submitted a quote well below the other builders, this is actually worryingly low, and most sensible customers would be concerned with such a low quote compared to the others.

The other 8 builders all quote similar fees which are most likely based on materials, time and expertise.

Do some research and look at what others are charging in your area.

Your location is also going to have a huge impact on how much you can and should be charging.

You would be able to charge a lot more if you are based in a big city like London or New York, these places have a higher cost of living and higher level of wage, so it goes without saying that the cost for entertainment would be increased as well.

Newmarket, the town where I live, at the time of writing, has a population of approximately 16,600, Newmarket is the third largest town in the county and very close to Cambridge with a population of approximately 123.900.

I spoke to quite a few magicians when writing this book and most said they would quote for 2 hours only and prices ranged from £250 - £600.

I generally quote for 3 hours (reception and wedding breakfast or evening party) and my fee within 1 hour of my home for the 3 hours is £500.

This places me in the upper section of local magician fees and this is a place I like to sit.

Some people would prefer to be the top charging, and some like to go as low as they can and again this is all personal and up to you.

The easiest way to work out your fee though is to make a list of what it costs you to do the show, including suit cleaning, playing cards, petrol, car maintenance, Tax, business cards and publicity material, website etc.

You will be amazed how quickly these things add up and you realise how much it actually costs to run a business.

Sell your services for the price that not only compensates you for your time and skill but is also reflected by the market value.

Deposits.
Whenever I take a booking I ask for a deposit, this is a sign of a commitment from the client to the supplier and likewise back to the client.

Some people do not like taking deposits, but I would say that I cannot remember taking a booking in the last 10 years at least when the client has not asked (before I can bring it up) about paying a deposit, it is expected.

Regardless of my fee I ask for a £50 deposit and as soon as I receive any payments I immediately email a receipt to the client detailing not only the payment they have just made but also the payments already made and the current balance loft to pay.

Additional Numbers.
Get the phone number for the best man/woman and chief bridesmaid so that any issues on the day can be dealt with, without harassing the B&G who will be stressed enough.

On the day payments.
I will always try to ensure that full payment is made before the day, however sometimes it will come down to payment on the day, if this is how you are getting the payment, then you need to ensure two things.

- Bring a receipt.
  This is really important, you need to keep on top of all payments etc, so make sure you have a receipt that is ready to be handed over when you receive the payment.

- Suggest the final payment is given to the best man/woman.
  The last thing you want to be doing is chasing the B&G around for that final payment so suggest the money or cheque is handed to the best man/woman to keep and look after.

  They are much less busy at the reception up until the speeches so you can easily sneak a couple of minutes with them and get the payment sorted.

Contracts.
Any business needs paperwork, so make sure you have correct paperwork ready to send out to clients.

If you use CRM software like Giggio, they have a feature to set up and send this and it works like a dream.

However, if you do not use this kind of system, you can easily make up your own and have it ready to send out as and when you need it.

The contract should feature all the information you have got from the client.

This should include their contact details, the information for the event and also your rider, which is a terms and conditions section.

My Contract lists everything clearly and in a manner that is easy to read and understand.

Alongside a contract you will need to generate an invoice and receipt to keep on top of any money transfers, deposits or payments.

Dear

Thank you so much for booking Wayne Goodman for your upcoming event, please find below the agreed confirmation.

If you are happy to confirm please just click reply and this will send the confirmation back to me with the word confirmed at the top.

Thank you again and I look forward to seeing you soon at the event.

CONFIRMED

www.waynegoodman.co.uk
07726 190078
9 Warrington Street, Newmarket, Suffolk, CB8 8BA
Company Registration Number - 2269802

Associate Member Inner Magic Circle with Silver Star

CONTRACT AND INVOICE NUMBER:|

Whilst every reasonable safeguard is assured, Wayne Goodman Entertainments will not be held responsible for any breach of contract by the Engager or by the Artiste.
This document reflects the legally binding verbal agreement already made.
BETWEEN THE ENGAGER:
CONTACT NUMBER:
CONTACT EMAIL:
AND THE ARTISTE: Wayne Goodman
Whereby the Engager engages Wayne Goodman and the Wayne Goodman accepts the engagement to present/appear as known as scheduled below:
DATE OF ENGAGEMENT(S):
VENUE:
TIMES:
EVENT:
TYPE OF SHOW:
TOTAL FEE: £

As you can see it has a simple layout with a brief thank you message above, then my personal information and finally the details of the booking.

The next section I have deleted is my bank information and then beneath that deleted section is the terms and conditions.

TERMS AND CONDITIONS OF CONTRACT:

1   CANCELLATIONS:

(i) Should 'The Engager' be the cancelling party he will be open to a claim by 'The Artiste' for the contracted fee plus all costs of recovery in the event of a dispute. Any prepayment or deposit paid by 'The Engager' will not be refundable.

(ii) In the event of Illness or Accident resulting in failure to complete the contract 'The Artiste' will notify 'The Engager' and Wayne Goodman Entertainments at the earliest opportunity and shall endeavour to find a replacement artiste at no extra cost to 'The Engager'

(iii) Should 'The Engager' decide to cancel within 30 Days of the show they will be required to pay 100% of the agreed fee (Plus all costs incurred). Should 'The Engager' decide to cancel within 60 days of the show they will be required to pay 60% of the agreed fee (Plus all costs incurred).

2   PROHIBIT:

'The Engager' may prohibit 'The Artistes' performance in part or in whole ('The Artiste' being ready, willing and able to appear) without giving any reason, provided that 'The Engager' pays 'the Artiste' the full contracted fee.

3.   PERFORMANCE & REST AREA:

If required 'The Engager' shall be responsible for ensuring a safe performance area/stage including access to electricity if required.

'The Engager' is also required to provide a changing/rest area if required by 'The Artiste'. Any changing rooms etc will be requested at the time of booking.

4.   ACCESS:

If Required 'The Engager' shall be responsible for ensuring that access is available to the venue for 'The Artiste' and his equipment in order that 'The Artiste' has sufficient time to set up and sound check equipment before the specified performance.

If possible a car park space should be reserved for the artiste.

5.   SAFETY:

'The Engager' shall ensure that no injury is caused to 'The Artiste' or any damage is caused to 'The Artistes' equipment due to the actions of guests or the negligence of 'The Engager'. Any damage and subsequent repairs/replacements will be the responsibility of 'The Engager'.

6.   PUBLIC LIABILITY INSURANCE:

'The Artiste' is covered with his/her own Public Liability Insurance.

Wayne Goodman Entertainments will not be held responsible for any death, injury or loss whatsoever. A copy of the PLI Certificate is available if required.

7.   PAYMENT:

Payments will be made before the event or on the day via bank transfer, cash or cheque or paypal. Overdue Payments will be subject to a penalty charge on a weekly basis at a rate of 8% above Bank Base Rate plus all costs of recovery.

This email and the information it contains may be privileged and/or confidential. It is for the intended addressee(s) only.

The unauthorised use, disclosure or copying of this email, or any information it contains is prohibited and could, in certain circumstances be a criminal offence.

If you are not the intended recipient please notifywayne@waynegoodman.co.uk immediately and delete the message from your system.

The rider covers all the information regarding the legal side of the booking including PLI. cancellations etc and this is another part of the job that you will need to look into and make your own decisions about.

The Wedding

Thinking back to my first wedding show is a real trip down memory lane, I am not sure who was more nervous the B&G or me, and it puts me in mind of the first ship I worked on, the MS Norsun, which sailed out of Hull in the north of the Uk and across the North Sea to Rotterdam in Holland.

As my car turned off the main road into the docks and I saw the ship for the first time, I was a little taken aback by how huge she was.

I had the same emotional reaction when I was at my first wedding.

Growing up I had not attended many weddings. I was astounded by the beauty of the occasion, the suits, the people, the venue and of course the bride, who shone as she entered the room.

Jump forward a few decades and add to that hundreds of weddings and the feelings have not changed one bit. I love the ambience, the feeling of a group of people all coming together to celebrate the union of families and the fact it is my job to make it the best day for everyone.

The wedding day is a very formal affair and for the B&G it begins as soon as they wake up.

I have seen loads of pictures of Brides in their rooms with their bridesmaids and Mums etc all wrapped up in dressing gowns and drinking champagne and prosecco and enjoying a celebratory breakfast.

On the flip side are the pictures of the Grooms with their best men and groomsmen, smoking cigars, having a beer and toasting the start of the special day.

The wedding day will follow a simple but strict running order and as a wedding supplier you need to know when and where you belong.

The running order of the day.
Every wedding is different, however this is the basic outline of the running of the wedding day.

Sometimes the speeches will occur before the Wedding Breakfast, which is becoming a more popular choice.

This choice enables the three speechmakers, normally the Father of the Bride, the Groom and the Bestman, to be able to relax and eat their food without the anxiety of having to make a speech afterwards.

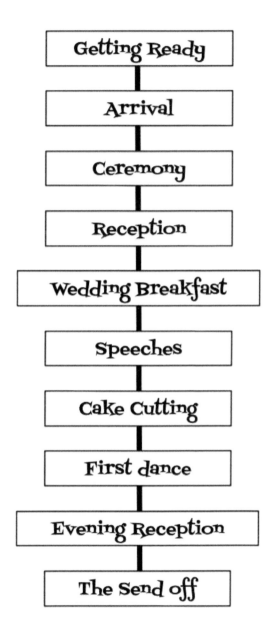

Getting Ready

Arrival

Ceremony

Reception

Wedding Breakfast

Speeches

Cake Cutting

First dance

Evening Reception

The Send off

Now we can look at the same timeline with our main times of interest highlighted.

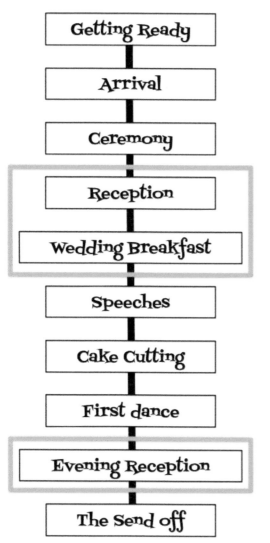

I will advise the B&G that these are the best times for me to be performing.

The Reception.
This is the part of the day that happens directly after the ceremony, it is also the time that is the most unstructured for the whole day.

The B&G will vanish with the photographer to get their wedding photos done, whilst the guests are left alone to have a drink and relax before the Wedding Breakfast starts.

Wedding Breakfast.
Guests are seated and the B&G make their big entrance, the whole happy couple now partake of their first meal as a wedded couple.

Evening Reception.
This is the evening party, usually with a disco or live music or both and is the most informal part of the day.

There will normally be an intake of new people to join the day guests but that does not always happen.

I will also offer either as an incentive or as an add-on that I can do a children's show during the speeches to keep the little ones entertained and busy.

The wedding.
A wedding is a huge event, involving hundreds of people all moving in different directions whilst trying to arrive at the same fixed point.

From the B&G and their wedding party, the wedding guests, the hospitality staff, kitchen staff, bar staff, cleaners, registrars, wedding suppliers and right in the middle is you, the wedding magician.

The wedding itself is a giant machine with so many moving parts, so it is important for you to know where you fit in and how to avoid clogging up the machine and stalling or stopping the day.

As a performer, you are uniquely placed to reap the gratitude and gratification for almost everything that is going on.

You become the ambassador for all the suppliers who are not there.

I was at a wedding and the mother of bride came up to me, hugged me and kissed me on the cheek and thanked me for such a beautiful performance, then, with tears in her eyes, thanked me for how beautiful the cake was, the decorations and the venue and as she hugged me again, she thanked me for everything that had been perfect.

I could have stopped her, told her that I had zero input with the cake making, decorations or how the venue was built, but I did not, instead I told her it was a pleasure and an honour for all the wedding suppliers to be a part of her daughters day, hugged her back and told her how beautiful everything had been.

I can not think of a wedding I have been to where the Bride or Groom has not come up to me and said, "it is all going so well, thank you so much".

Afterwards I make sure to message the other suppliers and pass on the relevant comments.

Part of a team.

You are an important part of the day but you are not the most important person there, so leave your ego in the car and get ready to be part of an amazing team of people all working together.

Know the team at the venue, make professional relationships with everyone you meet, you never know where it may lead.

The first time I worked at a local wedding venue I made friends with the barman, I showed him some tricks and began a friendship that has lasted to this current day.

Within a couple of years he moved up the ranks to head barman and then when he left that venue and went to work for another wedding venue as head of the wedding team, guess who put at the top of the wedding recommendations list.

Another similar story from the first wedding venue, there was a girl called Anna, she was a server, cleaner and general staff member, she was a great girl and hard worker and I would see her at every wedding over the next few years before she finished working at the venue and off to college.

Being nice to all the hospitality staff resulted in Anna remembering me and booking me for her own wedding in 2018.

I do honestly feel that because I did not place myself or my own importance above any of the staff at the venue or the other suppliers, and through the professional friendships I have made over the years, a large portion of my workload has been thanks to these people through recommending me or advising their clients that I am a supplier they should seriously consider.

Attire

There is an old saying that says,

"Dress for the job you want, not for the job you have".

Which is why I go everywhere dressed as Superman, joking aside, this works fine when you work in the corporate world, however for entertainment I would change it to,

"Dress appropriately for the show that you are doing".

This means if you are doing a children's show then a bright colourful outfit is more appropriate than a tuxedo, although I have seen plenty wear a tux for a children's show.

Likewise, unless your character dictates or it has been requested, wearing a multicoloured sparkly dungaree jumpsuit is not the most ideal outfit for a wedding.

Choosing your outfit.
A simple browse through social media for wedding magicians will throw up a host of different styles and outfits, some wear a smart suit, some have a more relaxed approach and it all depends on your own style and personality.

I saw one magician picture, he was wearing dark trousers, a white shirt with braces over the top and he had the sleeves to the shirt folded back.

To be honest, the look was smart but relaxed and I loved his style, but I know it would not suit me.

I wear a light coloured three piece suit with a smart double collared shirt and no tie, this works for me, I am smart but also relaxed, and most importantly I do not look like an usher or a guest.

My friend Andy Chase, who is an amazing wedding magician, will enquire at the time of booking on the B&G colour choices, this means he is able to make choices on what he wears so he does not blend in with the ushers, groomsmen etc.

This grey suit is one of my favorites. It is bright enough to make me stand out, but not loud enough to make me become a spectacle or overshadow everything else.

I remember when I first started in magic I was told I had to wear either a Tuxedo or dinner jacket with a bow tie and if possible a cummerbund, which I did, but not for long.

The cummerbund and dinner jacket soon vanished, although the bowtie did stick around for a little while.

Honestly, I still have that fan of cards. This is me circa 1992.

Clothes maketh the Man (or Woman).
Looking the part on the day does not just mean wearing a nice suit, or a cool outfit.

Personal hygiene is so important, make sure you have had a shave, had a shower etc, you are going to be working in close proximity to people and you do not want to be putting people off because of bad body odour.

Clean hair, teeth and fingernails are imperative, as is making sure you are wearing clean clothes.

Do not overlook the shoes.
Your shoes are another important part of your outfit so make sure they fit with the rest of your style.

Give them a good clean too before you start.

I have a shoes upkeep bag in my car with a brush and cloth to give them a quick buff up if required before I start.

I also do not travel to my shows in my work shoes but instead take them in a separate bag and put them on when I get to the venue.

Personality of clothing.
I believe when it comes to what you wear you should be guided by your personality, allow the clothes to be an extension of who you are and what you are doing.

I have met loads of magicians who have embraced this thinking and have developed characters or alter-egos to do this.

I know magicians who dress and act like.
- Gandalf or Dumbledore with flowing gowns, hats and beards.
- Steampunk.
- Noir.
- Comical suits like Opposuits etc.
- Movie and TV look-alikes.

All of these work for them, because they have made them work for them, so choose who you want to be, and then choose the outfit to suit.

This is the amazing Joel Dickinson, his suit is smart and modern and he stands out but he does not overshadow the other guests or the B&G.

Your attire is as important as your effects, you do not want it to let you down when you work so hard on every other aspect of your presence.

Your attire should be appropriate, suit your style and complement your personality. It should also be comfortable, remember you will be wearing it for a few hours at least and if it is uncomfortable it will affect your performances.

The Reception

The big day has arrived, you are booked for the reception mix and mingle and you have arrived at the venue, set up and ready to start, the couple are still in the ceremony and the staff are busy sorting the canapes and reception drinks.

The reception is normally the only part of the day that is unstructured, most couples, during the planning stage, presume the guests will be fine, being left alone whilst they have their photographs done.

In reality, the guests will not mix and mingle, they will normally converge into small groups and have a few drinks until it is time to be seated for the wedding breakfast.

The Flow.
noun

plural noun: **flows**
1. 1.
    the action or fact of moving along in a steady, continuous stream.

Throughout this book I will be talking about the flow of the day.

The wedding day, like a stream, should flow smoothly from the start to the end.

If you build into a free flowing stream lots of obstacles and dams, then you disrupt that smooth flow of water and slow it right down.

If you have a day that is fragmented or disjointed then the flow will be interrupted and the wedding guests will not get the smooth experience of the day that is intended.

The wedding day is full of structure and formality, so you need to make sure that anything you add to the day will allow for a smooth transition from one part of the formality to the next.

The Reception.
This is the time I will always recommend to a B&G as the most important time to have me at the wedding. This is the start of the day and you want to make sure that after the high of the ceremony, it does not dip before you reach the wedding breakfast.

The flow of the evening should be a steady incline, starting from when guests arrive through to the end of the night.

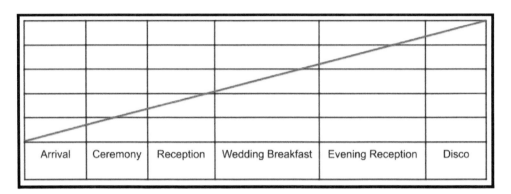

| Arrival | Ceremony | Reception | Wedding Breakfast | Evening Reception | Disco |

This image shows how it flows in a gentle but steady rise from beginning to end, and as you can see, the flow of the day should be a single and straight line from lowest to highest.

It is unfortunate that it is the bride and groom who will unintentionally sabotage their own perfect day by not planning properly for the reception, they incorrectly presume that as they will be busy with their photographs, that the rest of the reception will be flowing smoothly in their absence.

This is something I will bring up in the initial meeting or at the wedding fayre and highlight the issue and then give them the solution, thus making sure that when they return to the reception, the guests will be engaged with what I am doing and the atmosphere and flow of the day will be climbing.

If you start the day properly and then have a lull when the reception is happening then the climb to the end of the night is not only steeper but also harder to climb.

Arrival	Ceremony	Reception	Wedding Breakfast	Evening Reception	Disco

This image perfectly illustrates the disruption of the smooth flow of the day and the overall effect it has.

You need to ensure that if you are going to be a part of this day, then you need to be a part that does not slow down or stall the day.

Fitting in.
Making sure you fit in with the running of the day is so important, you need to make your presence known, but in a way that complements the day not complicates it.

I am naturally quite loud, and this is a distinct advantage when I am on stage or doing outdoor shows and fetes but at a wedding I need to be seen and heard but not at the expense of the day.

I do this by fitting in with the rest of the reception party, I will approach a few people in a quieter, more reserved manner, introduce myself and then show them a couple of effects.

At the same time, I will be encouraging other people, who are standing nearby, to approach and watch as well.

As the group around me builds, so does my volume and my personality, but not too extreme, just to the point of being above the rest of the group, so that other people will also be attracted to come over and see what is happening.

Once I have reached a good number of spectators, which for me is about 15 people, but of course will depend on the size of the reception party, I will finish up, inform them that I am there for the day and will come back over shortly, at this point, I will move on and start another group of watchers in another part of the reception party.

Photo time.
The main reason for the reception is to cover the time whilst the B&G are away having their wedding photographs and thus unlike other close up magic arena's, a wedding does have moments of requirement that may interrupt your performance.

I could be performing for a small group of people, for example, and one or more of them is "required" to go off and become part of the photos that are happening.

This can have a massive impact on what you are doing, so in an attempt to try and counterbalance this, for walk around, I will do effects that can be stopped at any moment without compromising my presence or stature.

In my walkabout I do a lot of manipulation with coins and Sharpies and if I am doing any card tricks, I will avoid anything that has a long or convoluted routine.

Being prepared for this, enables me to act accordingly, instead of being surprised by it.

The B&G will normally aim to be gone for a large section of the reception but will most likely make an appearance at some point, they will normally be followed around by the photographer who will be snapping more pictures as well as snapping some of the guests too.

I will always make sure that the photographer knows I am there and this normally leads to me getting a few pictures of me in action from the day.

The Magic.
Depending on the booking you have agreed, you could be at the wedding for upto three different parts of the day.

- The drinks reception.
- The wedding breakfast.
- The evening reception.

This means you will require up to three different sets of effects so as not to repeat.

Most of the guests will be outside, (weather permitting), or around the bar area, and most people will either be sat at small tables or stood in small groups.

This means I need to ensure the magic I will be performing can be done in the hands and does not require a table to use.

Effects I perform at this stage will include cards, coins, business cards, sponge balls etc, everything must fit in my pockets, must be highly visible and not require a table.

For this I like effects like "Misled" or "Sharpie through card", "Bill switch", a small version of "Professors nightmare", Daryl's "The whole thing", "Coins across", and other similar effects.

I also have a few small effects using my own business cards etc.

Every effect or routine I use is carefully considered, you must remember that in the reception area you can end up totally surrounded by guests, so you need to ensure you can maintain control over what the spectators can and should see and what they should not be able to see as well.

Considering my list of effects above I know that routines like "Misled" or "The whole thing" could be compromised if I get surrounded etc so I am ready to drop them and do something else if required.

Ignoring the Bride and Groom.

Once the B&G have arrived at the reception, I will aim to ignore them for as long as possible.

Now I should state here that this tactic is discussed with the B&G during the planning stage and is a strategy that really makes good use of me for the benefit of the B&G.

So why do I want to ignore the B&G?

There is more than one answer to this, so I will break it down here into a few separate reasons.

Once the B&G are back at the reception they are going to be inundated with people wanting to speak to them, congratulate them and of course spend some time with them.

My first job is to keep people occupied so that the B&G can firstly relax and speak to people, but also so they do not have the entire wedding party rushing for them. By ignoring the B&G, I am enabling them to speak to the people they want or need to talk to, such as guests who have travelled a long distance or who may have contributed to the day.

Some venues have a small side room prepared with a glass of champagne and a plate of canapes, so that the B&G can escape for five minutes, refresh themselves and then re-enter the reception ready to face the party.

Now all that being what it is, if the Bride or Groom come over and stand and watch me perform I am not going to send them away or move off, I just do not actively seek them out during this part of the reception.

Once again, and this is the important part, this whole strategy is discussed and explained with the B&G during the planning stage.

I also make it clear that once they are seated for the wedding breakfast they will get a special show that only the top table ever gets to see.

The Missing Bride and Groom.
Sometimes during the reception, it will be nearing the time for everyone to be seated, and the B&G are nowhere to be found.

This can be a cause for concern, however if you are prepared for it, then it should not be a problem.

When I take the booking, I always make sure I allow for any - on the day - situations, and make sure that should any arise, I am not leaving at the key moment they may need me to be there.

When it comes to weddings I always book for the event and not for the amount of time.

This actually happens a lot more than you would expect and the cause for this late return is normally down to either the photographer or circumstance.

If it is the photographer's fault then that is on them, however more often than not it is due to a circumstance of the day.

I have heard hundreds of reasons why the B&G are late back but my favorite three are,

- They found a man with a classic, open top sports car and he allowed them to sit in the car and pose for a few extra pictures.

- The sun was behind a tree and was shining through the leaves and branches and it looked really amazing so they used it as a backdrop for a few extra photographs.

- The B&G fell down a well and had to call the fire brigade to pull them out. They had been posing on the edge of the well, when the Bride fell in, and in a gallant attempt to save her, the Groom fell in after her.
Luckily no one was hurt, and it made for a very funny story when they returned to the reception.

Make the most of the reception.
The reception is a brilliant time to perform, everyone is happy, hopefully they have not had too much to drink and it is a great opportunity to really showcase and show off your skills, personality and ability.

I love the reception, I love performing for people and the reception is a brilliant place to really work some quality material, it also allows me to set myself up for the wedding breakfast as well as the evening reception if I am booked for both.

The Wedding Breakfast

The one question I get asked a lot when chatting to the B&G is,

"Why is it called the wedding breakfast?"

The name comes from the 1700's when traditionally the ceremony was held after mass, the whole wedding party would not eat for the entirety of the wedding day until after the ceremony and so when they sat down to eat, it would be the first meal of the day, hence the wedding breakfast.

It is also the first meal eaten as a new combined family.

Speeches.
Normally the wedding breakfast would be immediately followed by the speeches however it has become more common to have the speeches before the breakfast, this allows the speech givers to enjoy the meal without the building anxiety of having to give a speech.

During the planning stages make sure you know if the speeches are happening before or after the meal so you can plan your time accordingly.

Table hopping.
The guests are sat and the food is about to be served, normally at a formal wedding breakfast there will be three courses and the order will be,

- Bride and Groom (sat at the top table).
- Top table (remainder of top table guests).
- Surrounding tables.
- Outer tables.

Before I start. I will speak to the venue staff and make sure I know the layout and also the order of the tables they are going to serve.

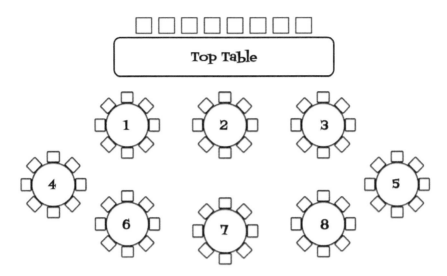

This is a common design for the layout of the seating plan, as you can see the top table is rightly placed at the top and then the other tables are layered,

- 1 - 2 - 3.   1st row.   Surrounding tables.
- 4 - 5.   2nd row.   Outer tables.
- 6 - 7 - 8.   3rd row.   Outer tables.

Normally seated at the top table will be,

- The Bride and Groom.
- The Bride's parents.
- The Groom's parents.
- The Bestman.
- Chief Bridesmaid.

Sometimes the top table may have other important guests, however the above list is a good representation of a normal set up.

Now I know the set up and I know that they will serve the top table then the other tables in order, I can plan my route around the room.

I do not want to approach tables 1 - 4 as they will be served their food pretty quickly, and as I know that table 8 will be the last table served, and therefore tables 6 - 8 will be waiting the longest, it makes sense for me to start there.

My aim is to get around all the tables, so I will generally work tables 8, 7, 6 and maybe 5 during the serving of the starters.

I do not like to do magic at the tables when they are eating, however during the starters I do break this rule if needed and will do effects that can be done in my hand and visual to the whole table such as the bill switch etc.

Once table 8 gets their starters, the top table will be either finished or about to finish, so I will head over to the top table at this point and do a quick effect for the whole table.

Serving the main course takes a little longer, so I will start at table 5 or 4 and continue working the tables again until all tables are eating.

During this part I will just move around the room working any tables that are not eating, up until they are served their food.

Once the top table has finished, and knowing that most venues will give the guests a little break between the main course and dessert, I now approach the top table to perform my special routines for the B&G.

Once the desserts are being served I will carry on working around the tables.

Table hopping 2.0.
I have found over the last 30+ years that I do work some aspects of close up / table hopping in a slightly different manner to how other performers work.

These ideas grew from my residencies and restaurant experience, which is also discussed in detail in my book, "The expert at the restaurant table".

Firstly I do not have a set routine, I have a number of effects on me that are specifically chosen or designed so that I can start, pause, stop and restart at any time.

This way of working gives me a lot of freedom and does not ruin my performance if something happens and I have to stop.

Secondly I very rarely work to a single table, even though I am performing, for example, to table 6, by positioning myself in the correct position I can also be seen by tables 4 and 1.

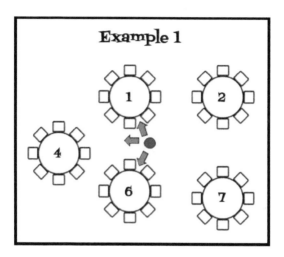

By shifting in my stance I can instead work for tables 6, 4 and 7.

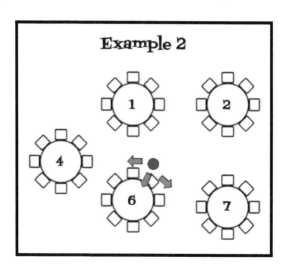

If you look at the whole seating plan you can easily see how multiple tables are visible from almost any position in the room.

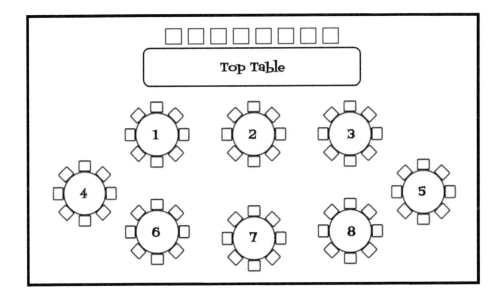

The Oddbins table.
I have often heard that organising the seating plan is one of the most stressful parts of planning a wedding. This is addressed in other chapters in this book but is also very relevant here too.

I make sure I know which table has the people on who have not been easily placed.

At these tables I will perform a few tricks that are chosen to encourage maximum participation so that everyone at the table is a part of the effect, routine or performance.

Getting everyone involved is a good idea at any and every table however at the oddbins table it is, in my opinion, a necessity, as I want them to be engaged and active when I leave the table, so that this one spark will encourage conversation that will carry them into the evening reception.

Disaster prevention.
You never know when something will happen that will stall or stop the running of the wedding day.

I have learnt to expect the unexpected, to be prepared for anything to happen, because it can and it will.

I was working one wedding venue, and just as they were preparing to serve the first few tables with the main course, the young girl working at the venue as a waitress dropped 10 - 12 plates on the floor of the kitchen, the caterers needed a few minutes to sort this problem and I offered to distract the audience from the delay.

How did I do this, well I used the same technique for another problem I encountered at another wedding.

I was at a wedding in January 2020, this was actually my last wedding before we hit the first Covid-19 Lockdown in the UK.

The wedding was for a friend of mine called Wez, and he has kindly given me permission to retell this story.

The wedding was a beautiful day in an amazing manor in Suffolk.

The wedding went off without a problem but once Wez returned to the reception he was hit by a crushing wave of nerves and anxiety about his wedding speech.

He literally spent the entire reception time in the wedding suite bathroom and could not face the breakfast or the thought of giving a speech to a group of people.

I spoke to Wez and made him feel a bit better with some anecdotes about jokes and when he said he needed a few minutes.

The way I solved both of these problems was to perform a quick stand up show for the whole room.

By offering Wez a quick 15 minute show, this would give him a chance to freshen up and I would warm the room up for him.

I went out and performed an off the cuff impromptu magic cabaret for the seated guests, (Twisting the arms, cards to pocket, Cigarette in jacket and finished with the four person suspension) and got the audience on their feet for the finale.

This was also the moment I welcomed the B&G into the room and Wez appeared, smiling and happy and went straight into his speech, which was always planned to be before the meal.

By being prepared I was able to step into the dilemma with a solution and every time I have done this, and to be honest I have done this a lot, the rest of the guests thought it was just another part of the day and were totally unaware that a problem even existed.

"Preparation is half the victory"

Evening Reception

The evening reception happens after the wedding breakfast with guests normally arriving during the speeches (if they are a little early) or shortly afterwards.

The B&G get a short time to meet and greet their new guests and then it is time to cut the cake and then the music starts with the first dance.

The evening party reception normally has a serving of more food but this is more formal and usually a buffet of sorts or sometimes something special like a fish and chip van or similar.

The evening reception is different from the day time reception for a number of reasons, mostly because it is less structured and a lot less formal and follows a similar running order of a big celebratory party.

The Magic.
Being booked for the evening reception means you will be performing mostly around groups of people and also maybe a few people who are seated.
Most venues will move the guests to a new area and clear the wedding breakfast tables, the new area will most likely have a lot less seating than the main dining area.

This means the material you perform should be similar to what you would use during the reception, by this I mean in the hands material as opposed to effects that require a table.

Plan what you are going to perform and even rotate material, I will sometimes plan to switch in and out effects throughout the evening so that I can ensure repeat groups etc see different material as the evening progresses.

Work out what is the best way to maximise your time and the effects you want to perform so that you are seen at your best.

One of the main reasons I love the evening reception is that it is a lot less formal and more relaxed, so you should be able to spend more time with the guests and a lot less time jumping from group to group.

I love performing longer routines or effects that are a little more complex, effects like Brian Caswell's "Trilogy" or Chris Congeaves "Roll" are brilliant for the evening reception, I know I can run the full routine with almost no chance of them being interrupted by some formality in the running order.

The band, the DJ and the increased volume.
The main entertainment during the evening reception will be the music, whether this comes from a disco or a live band and if you are booked for the evening reception, this will be your main nemesis.

Unfortunately, this is a battle you are neither equipped for, nor capable of winning and so you need to be prepared to work around the problem instead of trying to take it head on.

I have spent many years working in bars, discos and venues with loud music but now I have neither the desire nor inclination to try and compete with the music.

I will spend some time in the bar area and around where everyone is, but I will also spend some of the time working in the areas of the venue where the music is not too loud and I can reign supreme as the master of the quieter zones.

There will always be places where people can go and sit and talk etc and I make sure I know where they are so I can work and be seen and heard.

If you have no issue working in a loud venue, then go for it, enjoy it and embrace the atmosphere etc. I had a blast working nightclubs and venues and as long as you keep it visual and showy then you should not have much of a problem.

The new guests.
The evening reception usually means evening guests, although this is not always the case, I have performed at quite a few weddings where there were no additional guests invited.

The evening guests, as stated, will normally arrive either during the speeches or immediately after and will be guided straight to the bar area to wait until the B&G and day guests evacuate the dining area.

If you are booked to entertain at both the day and evening reception, then you will not have to work so hard to be accepted into the proceedings.

The daytime guests will be hyped up by what they have seen and will be excited to show you off to their friends and family who have just arrived.

If you have only been booked for the evening reception, then you will have to work the crowd like any other party or event.

Children at the Wedding

Child guests.
I knew when I started this chapter that it would be a big chapter, and to be honest I did consider writing this as a separate book as the amount of information I could write could and would fill a whole book, maybe that's the next project.

For this book though, I am going to cover the essential information and look at a couple of ideas and concepts I have worked on when entertaining children at weddings.

This is NOT a chapter about doing children's shows at a wedding, although I will cover that later in the chapter, this is about when you approach a group or a table and there are children at the table.

If there are infants, aged 18m - 3years, they will tend to be either very clingy to their parents and therefore not much interest in what you, or anyone else is doing, or they are too busy running around etc and thus not part of my concern for the performance.

Sometimes you will get a little one who shows some interest, and I will acknowledge them and say "Hi" maybe do a quick vanish of something off the table before carrying on with the rest of the routine.

If the child is aged 4 - 9, then this is the age group I would refer to as Children at the wedding, this is the age that will want to have some attention and want to assist with the effect and get involved, don't worry, they will soon let you know this.

The final age group is the 10+, at that age they will not be interested in the normal concept of children's magic and will be more entertained and engaged by the same effects I perform for the adults.

Once a child is heading towards secondary level education, their attitudes, likes and dislikes etc will change and they will want to be seen as more grown up by everyone else.

Children at the wedding.

A wedding is a special occasion and also, very much, a family occasion that means you will, at most weddings, be required to entertain at a group or table that has children present.

I know that some performers are scared of performing for children because they have a tendency to make noise, speak out and generally disrupt the show and whilst this is true, if you deal with them in a professional manner, albeit a fun professional manner, then you should be alright.

Weddings can be a bit of a parabox, they are a fun celebration and party but still full of formality and structure, they are a family event but not really child friendly. Children will be told to stand still, sit quietly, not run around etc and so when a magician appears and offers some magic for them, of course they are going to want to get involved.

A little understanding and forethought, being prepared and a little patience will endear you with the adults as well as keeping control over the whole table.

I love doing magic for children, not just in my kids' shows but also in restaurants and at weddings.

Children really do make the magic real, they believe, not like an adult who wants to believe, they really do believe and the wonder in a child's eye and the gasp and cheer of a child watching magic is what makes it real for me too.

I remember working at the North Wales Magic Circle Presidents dinner in 2016, I was booked to compere and also to do an act and my daughter Charlee was also invited to attend too.

That night she was given a front row seat and loved the show, but my favorite part of the show was watching her enjoy the amazing Romany doing her act.

To say she was captivated or enthralled would be a total understatement and as Romany was on stage doing her thing, every time a birdcage appeared, Charlee's hands flew into the air for a rapturous round of applause.

Romany was the star of the show and Charlee talked non stop about her for the entire 4 hour drive home.

This is the impact we have or can have on children in the audience, even if you are not performing directly for them.

Romany performed her normal act, which is not an act aimed at children, and yet she still connected with Charlee and the other children present.

When I work at tables or groups of people where children are present I want to elicit the same response to my material, I want the Children to be raving about me long after I leave the tables.

I want the Children to be writing thank you letters to the B&G thanking them for the invite to the wedding and mentioning me in the letters.

Change your mindset, not your routines.
So how do you do this? How do you make this kind of connection with the children present?

The answer is so easy and yet missed by so many performers.

You do it the same way you would with a group of adults.

You treat them with respect and in a professional manner that is appropriate for the surroundings you are in.

I am not saying you should start hitting yourself over the head with a magic wand, in fact I am not even suggesting that you use a magic wand, (unless you already do).

What I am suggesting is that you interact with everyone in the same manner.

Now you may need to adjust your material or presentation for the children present and make it more understandable so they can appreciate it, or perform an extra trick just for them, but whatever you do, if you include them, rather than exclude them, you will get a much richer response from the whole table.

There are some amazing magicians in the community, like Oliver Graham (Magic Olly), that really grasp the concept of blurring the lines between children's magic and family magic, ensuring that no matter the effect, it will be watched and enjoyed by anyone of any age.

Oliver is a brilliant performer who has worked the last 15-20 years at Centre Parcs in Norfolk entertaining both close up and stage for every age group imaginable. His style is to take an effect or routine, like russian roulette, and make it suitable and enjoyable for children to enjoy.

If you have not seen Olly's family russian roulette then you are definitely missing out.

The other side to the coin is magicians like Paul Marlow (Taz), who instead takes a children's effect and makes it suitable for family performances.

Both these magicians use their skill set to enhance their shows in different ways to achieve the same goal.

I have watched other performers at events, weddings and restaurants and even at children's shows I have attended, and I realised that the performers who really struggle with children are the ones who do not talk TOO the child, but instead talk DOWN to the child.

Speak to the children how you would like to be spoken to by them, if you are rude and ignore them, then do not expect them to respect you, if you are nice and polite and act in a professional manner, they will reciprocate.

Of course some children can be horrible, spoilt, annoying, rude and disruptive, but then, so can some adults.

I once heard a magician discussing this and he said that he would ignore any child as he was not there to entertain children, he said at one wedding the boy at the table was getting louder and more annoying because he was ignored by the magician.

I asked the magician how he would feel if someone came to a table he was at and started talking and entertaining everyone but completely ignored him? How would he feel if he was treated as being invisible and just rudely ignored?

My point was that if you are rude to someone, regardless of age, they are not going to be enamored by them.

My other contention with this magician was that he was not there to entertain the children, when I am booked to perform at a wedding, I am booked to entertain all the guests, young and old, and as a professional I would be expected to do so.

I have a real blast when I perform for the children. I love to steal stuff off the table that they may have and then produce it during the show.

These pictures perfectly tell the story of what I am doing and the impact it has on those watching, not only for the children but also for the adults at the table too.

The bottom two pictures feature me doing two tricks that are not children's tricks, the boy with the glasses is assisting me with the end of my card routine and is holding the super heavy Moby Deck for the finale.

The girl has just found a cross on her hand that has travelled from her mothers hand aka Double Cross by Mark Southworth.

Two effects that emphasize the fact that you do not have to change or make any major adjustments on your performance.

What effects are suitable?
As stated above, you do not really need to change much at all, however there are some effects that immediately spring to mind that are worth a mention.

Sponge Balls.
Love them or hate them, a good sponge ball routine is worth its weight in gold and I never perform without mine. They are great for children and adults and although they have diminished in popularity over the last few years, for me they are an essential part of my toolbox.

Coins / Cards across.
A brilliant routine that utilises multiple spectators and is also nice and easy to follow for the younger members of the group.

Fork bending.
This is one of my all time favourite routines and one that works perfectly well for any age group, however if I am performing for families, I will tailor my routine so that it appears that the child is performing the magic and bending the cutlery.

Torn & Restored.
Card, paper napkin, sugar packet, the list is endless, but it is a nice and direct routine that is great for all ages and will really have an impact.

These are, of course, just suggestions, and like I have put previously, in reality you do not need to change anything except maybe the approach and a tweak or two to the presentation.

Every group is bespoke and has a different approach, if you were about to entertain a group of older ladies your approach would be different than performing for a group of rugby players, now change the scenario again to a family group with children present.

Children's magic during the speeches.
The speeches are quite a stressful time for the speech givers, add to this, that the speeches normally happen after the meal, after the children have been seated for over an hour, all of this can be the catalyst for the children to become disruptive and a distraction for the whole room.

This is why I offer, as an extra, a 20 - 30 minute children's show, that will keep the children occupied and entertained while the speeches are happening.

This is added on as an extra for the couple, but to be honest I keep my kids show in the car just in case I need it anyways.

I will discuss this at the time of the booking and tell them the cost for the children's magic show at this point, if they decide they want it, then I add it onto the total fee at the time of booking.

If however, they decide they do not want it, then I inform them they can always book it later on or on the day (timings permitting) if they decide it is needed.

For most weddings I do not bring in sound equipment or a huge set up, rather keeping this performance small and more contained, if there are going to be a large number of children then I will bring a smaller version of my full kids show to accommodate this.

I will always insist that at least one parent is with me when I am doing this side show, I am not a babysitter and I am not there to be responsible for the children, this has never been an issue and i usually end up with a couple of adults, mostly those ones who do not want to watch the speeches either.

Wedding activity books for Children.
The wedding activity book is something I designed as another addon for the B&G. Each book is A4 in size and contains pictures to colour in, puzzles to complete and activities that will keep the children busy during the wedding breakfast.

I also have similar books for circuses (two of my friends own their own circus and I designed the books for them) and also a magic one for my children's shows.

The book is available in two formats, the B&G can order preprinted versions from my Lulu bookshop,

www.lulu.com/spotlight/waynegoodman

The book is also available as a FREE download from my website, the B&G can email me through the website and request the book and I will email it to them, so they can print it themselves.

In my experience, most B&G do not want the hassle of printing XXX numbers of books and most will order the books from me for the day.

Here are a small selection of pages from the activity books,

Every page has my contact details and I have space on the pack cover to add all my contact information too.

These books are available to buy so you can offer them to your own clients.

I can add your own contact details too.

If you are interested then contact me at wayne@waynegoodman.co.uk.

The Bride & Groom

The wedding day is their day, everything that has happened, everyone who has attended and every photo that has been taken, is all because of them.

They have been smiled at, adored, adorned with gifts and cards and flowers and love, and now it is your turn to attend to the stars of the day.

As mentioned in the Reception chapter, during the drinks mix and mingle I do not actively seek out the B&G, nor do I perform anything special for them, if they do come over at this stage I will just perform my usual material for them and the guests watching.

Once they are sat at the top table, however, the game changes and I am prepared for some special routines just for them.

I have two sets of routines for the top table.

The first set is one that I will perform to everyone at the top table, this will include the parents, best man and chief bridesmaid as well as the Bride and Groom.

This first set is made up of effects that use more than one spectator, so I can incorporate a presentation that brings the families together. If I use the Bride's Father and the Groom's Mother or vice versa, or both Dads or Mums then it creates a unity, a bond between them.

I get a lot of letters and emails from couples, who state that when the families all get together, the tricks I did for them are always a subject of conversation, which is amazing to hear but also amplifies my credibility towards making their wedding day as special and as magical as I can.

My second set is exclusively for the Bride and Groom, although I perform it in a manner that others may watch, the effects are aimed directly at them.

In this set I will perform a number of routines that I only ever perform at weddings and only for the B&G, so if you see me performing at a birthday or a corporate event etc you will not see me performing these routines.

This is not to say I do not have variations for other events, such as Double Cross by Mark Southworth, in my everyday set I have the cross jump from hand to hand etc, however at the top table I have the alternative stamper, and so I draw a heart on the grooms hand and have it jumps to the brides.

The B&G set for me is a special thank you to the couple, it's the kiss at the end of a text from your partner or the £5 in the card from your Nan, it is a way of ending with a big finish and showing that being that has been special for you as well as for them.

The old saying is, "Save the best till last" and here you really are, you are saving the best, most special material, the best effects, the most amazing magic for the most amazing people.

These effects will be the ones that everyone will talk about afterwards, and people will want to see and examine the gifts you leave behind.

The effects I do, I will teach in the last section of this book, and you may like them, you may love them, you may decide to perform them, or you may not and make your own, but do not ignore this moment in the day, as it is the moment that everyone has been heading towards.

Creating lasting memories.
Most events will have someone snapping photographs, or will encourage guests to take pictures and upload them to social media for everyone to see and enjoy.

A wedding is one of only a few occasions when you have a dedicated photographer to capture the whole event.

The photographer is responsible for capturing the special moments of the day, but all the wedding suppliers have the responsibility to create those special moments that need to be captured.

The cake is a visual masterpiece, the dress is beyond amazing and the flowers bring the venue to life with colour and beauty.

That means when you perform you have to be at the top of your game, every wedding should end with you leaving and thinking,

"That was the best show I have ever done".

The good news is that you are already in a winning position, the booking is complete, the room loves you, the B&G already loved you and your style otherwise they would not have trusted you with the most important day of their lives, and now you just have to put the cherry on the top.

So no Pressure.

On the next couple of pages I have shared a couple of quotes from B&G that I have worked for.

I chose these quotes above the others because I felt they highlighted the main messages I have been talking about throughout the whole book.

> # "Wayne was excellent at keeping our guests entertained after dinner!
> ## Everyone has said how fantastic he was and that it was one of the highlights of the day.
> ## Not cheesy and predictable like many wedding entertainers, and amused both the children and the adults!
> ## Perfect!"

"Wayne was excellent.
He rotated around our wedding party throughout the reception, everyone loved it.
He also spent time going around the tables during the wedding breakfast, not at all intrusive. For those that were on tables where they didn't know everyone, it gave them something to talk about."

"Wayne was the consummate professional. Performing close to magic tricks for everyone. He appealed to all age groups 3 years - 80 years! He held a captive audience & was extremely good value for money!"

"I knew I wanted Wayne for our wedding within about 30 seconds of meeting him.
A true professional, Wayne is very talented, professional and frankly, hilarious. Our guests absolutely loved him and I'm just disappointed I don't get to have another wedding so I can book him again!!!"

"Wayne was absolutely Brilliant.
His services was so personal.
Absolutely everybody loved his performance.
The children were in awe of him the whole evening. It was a wonderful ice breaker for people that didn't know each other.
He was punctual, smart, very very funny and just an all round great guy."

The Magic

This is the first time I have written up some of these effects, but despite their new found place in print, these have been a major part of my wedding day magic for the last fifteen years or so, some even longer.

I have a number of effects that I love performing at weddings including some of my own original effects, some of which have been released commercially like "Lord of the Bling", my comedy version of the classic ring flight and available from Magic box in Newcastle, www.magicbox.uk.com/product/lord-of-the-bling

I also love performing tricks like

- Joe Porper's Ghostly Linking Finger Rings.
- Dave Penn's Refraction.
- Matthew Wright's RSVP box.
- Gary James Pro-Secco Deluxe.

All these effects are visual, have great magical content and fit perfectly into my themes and routines for a wedding day show.

I like to create my own effects, ideas and concepts too so over the next few pages I am going to explain some ideas, routines and effects that have been a staple of my performances for as long as I have done weddings.

I hope you enjoy them and get some use from them. They have served me well and now I hope they will do the same for you.

Magic at the Tables

Wedding tables are usually covered in small decorations made to brighten up, what is otherwise, a normal dinner table setting.

I love performing with items on the table, so I will regularly use items such as,

- Cutlery.
  Fork bending or Spoon-a-round by Axel Hecklau

- Wine glass.
  Refraction is a great effect but better for the top table.

- Torn and Restored Napkin.

- Salt pour.

- Silk to Chocolate.
  This is a new version of the classic silk to egg, except the silk ends up in a Ferrero Rocher, this means no mess or danger of breaking the egg and can be done table to table.

There are so many effects available, which have been designed to be used in a restaurant setting which is brilliant, but I love the effects I can perform that are a little more off the cuff and seem impromptu.

Table decorations.
You will find a thousand different small decorations such as acrylic diamonds, wooden hearts, engraved or burnt with a message or sometimes just plain, love words and the list goes on and on and on.

The decorations are normally scattered across the table after the table is set and opens up the possibilities for some amazing magic.

I describe one such effect in detail in another chapter of this book.

With a little imagination plus a small amount of preparation you can perform some unique, seemingly off the cuff magic at the tables.

Broken Love.
One frequent find at the tables is a broken decoration, such as a wooden word. If you can not find a broken one, then they are quite easy to snap in half yourself ready for the trick.

These small wooden decorations are beautiful and elegant but do break quite easily.

I will have a number of unbroken copies in my pocket ready to perform with.

I will take the broken word and show it to the audience, I will make a quip about how it does not represent the day and then proceed to restore it back to an unbroken decoration.

This is a brilliant, quick and visual effect that really looks off the cuff and amazing.

My heart will go on.
This quick trick requires a small amount of preparation, but is well worth it. I bought a number of small clear acrylic hearts from ebay, they cost around £10 for a dozen or so and are small enough to finger palm.

If there are small diamonds scattered across the table, I will scoop up a few and slowly drop them into my hand which I have made into a fist.

Inside the fist I have already placed the diamond and a thumbtip.

When I open my hand all the tiny diamonds have now transformed into a heart.

I will either hand the heart out to someone on the table or do a false transfer and immediately change them back into the small diamonds.

Wine Glasses.
Alongside great wine glass effects, do not overlook the cheeky gags and minor effects you can perform.

One of my all time favourites is to pick up a wine glass, in the action of moving it to avoid knocking it over, or in case I spill it, and as I do the glass stem breaks and the base of the glass falls to the table.

You freeze, look horrified, pick up the broken piece and then, restore it to the base of the glass.

You can now place the glass back down and carry on.

BE WARNED - as you place the glass back down, EVERYONE will reach for it to examine it and check it out.

I perform this action as if I have done nothing and do not bring any attention to it. The required gimmick for this is available from select magic dealers but to save you a search you can get it from Propdog here,

www.propdog.co.uk/broken-restored-wine-glass

Creating your own.
New decorations and items are always being added to wedding suppliers options and I can not think of a single time I have been to a wedding and not seen a new item on the tables or around the venue.

These small effects may seem inconsequential in the grand scheme of things, however, they are usually the ones that will garner the most reactions, mostly because they appear to be completely unplanned.

I get so many comments about the broken wine glass, it is now permanently in my pocket when I am working at any gig.

Have fun creating your own.

Look Sharp

Anniversary Edition

It was around 2008 when I released Look Sharp with Alakazam to the world wide magic community and even to this day not a month goes by that I do not get one or two messages on social media or email telling me how much the message sender loves look sharp and how they use it at every gig.

This really means a lot to me, it is very humbling to know that something I created is being used day in and day out all over the world.

In 2021, alongside the amazing Peter Nardi and the Alakazam Magic team, I will be rereleasing Look Sharp and alongside the normal effect and gimmick, we are also releasing a new version, based on an idea from Richard Furzer that is based around the concept of Anniversary Waltz meets Look Sharp.

Check out the alakazam website for more details. *www.alakazam.co.uk*

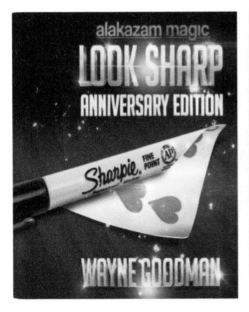

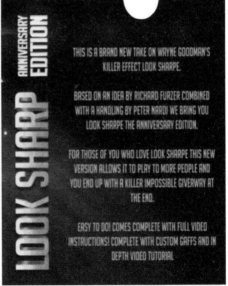

AC Deck of cards

This is an amazing concept that was shared with me by the brilliant UK magician Andy Chase.

The idea is to get a photo of the bride and groom and then have that image printed onto the back of a deck of cards.

There are thousands of sites offering this service that you can find through a simple google search.

Prices depend on where you look for them, but I found a few at places like Boots and Personalised Playing Cards Ltd for about £7.99 a pack.

What better way to bring some magic to the wedding than with a deck of cards with the bride and groom on them.

This was a deck of cards I got for a couple, this was the digital image they sent me as proof of the finished item.

The cards always get a huge reaction and I leave them with the B&G at the end of the wedding as a special keepsake for their special day.

Andy told me that sometimes he would use this deck of cards just at the top table for the routines for the B&G and other times he would just present the cards as a gift when he reached the top table.

Either way this is a brilliant idea and one that will be remembered for a long time after the wedding.

When I present the cards to the B&G I will always crack a joke like,

"These cards are a gift from me to you, you can take them on the honeymoon, you know, play some cards if you have nothing better to do."

Magicians will go through 500 decks of cards a year and think nothing of it, however normal people tend to keep cards for years and if it has the added value of being related to their wedding day, these cards could be with them a lifetime.

WG Deck of Cards

Another idea for a deck of cards is something I have been doing for around 20 years at weddings.

Normally at shows, when a spectator signs a card, I allow the spectator to keep the card as a keepsake.

At weddings I always have the spectator sign 2 cards, one for the trick and another from another deck but signed to the B&G with a message etc.

Once I have the deck completely signed, (usually on both sides) I present it to the B&G as an extra surprise gift for them.

I will use a normal deck of cards for this, usually red back cards are better as the writing shows up better on a red back than a blue back.

If I have any, I also use double blank cards and have the messages done on both sides too.

A great idea for this is also to do a deck switch and have the B&G's signed cards appear amongst all their guests' signed cards.

The guests love signing the cards and as you can see from the picture below the B&G loved the surprise deck of cards and the lovely messages they can read again and again.

The Interaction

Wedding edition

The interaction is a routine I released in 2020. This is a fantastic principle that allows me to control all the spectators to choose the same option.

In the package I sell you receive a number of prepared images that can be printed for a number of shows including,

- Birthday parties that end with everyone landing on and singing "Happy Birthday".
- Christmas parties that end with everyone landing on santa.
- Healthy eating.
- Superheroes.
- Movie posters.

Amongst many others.

I have created many versions of this effect but it stemmed from this version, which is the wedding edition.

I have been informed that the principle is based on a similar principle by Martin Gardiner.

In this chapter though I am going to share the wedding image and How I use it.

The Interaction
by
Wayne Goodman

For over 20 years Wayne Goodman has presented his Interaction effects in almost every performing arena, from stage shows to trade shows, kids shows to weddings.

Wayne has produced multiple variations and for the first time shares some of his designs and presentation ideas for you to adapt and perform. You receive multiple boards ready to be printed or sent digitally as well as a blank board for you to customise.

Effect:
The whole audience follows some basic instructions to randomly land on one of 12 different squares. The magician shows that they have all landed on the same square. The one predicted.

Download now for £20

wayne@waynegoodman.co.uk

Effect:
A brilliant routine that builds to the introduction of the Bride & Groom.

Required.
The effect requires the artwork and download of the interaction which you can purchase by contacting wayne@waynegoodman.co.uk.

This is the front of the postcard, and all the cards are laid with this side upwards.

This is the back design of the postcard with the interaction board printed on.

This is my postcard which features me on the top right hand corner, however the commercially released version has another image in that position.

It also comes with three different end results.

- Bride & Groom.
- Bride & Bride.
- Groom & Groom.

Routine.
I place one card at every seating place before I start.

Every wedding guest heads to their seats at the wedding breakfast and finds a postcard at their position. On the first side is my wedding contact information and on the reverse side is a small chart that resembles a wedding bingo board.

When it becomes time to introduce the B&G to the room, I will take control of the guests and ask them to pick up the postcard and turn it over.

I ask them to follow a set of instructions as they move around the board until they end up on a seemingly random position on the board.

I now ask everyone to stand up, and when I name one of the positions, If I am correct, then they should all applaud loudly.

I now state confidently, "You are on the BRIDE & GROOM"

As I state this, and as everyone starts to clap, the B&G enter the room.

Thoughts.
I love this routine as not only does it allow me to introduce the B&G in a novel and magical manner, it also enables me to make sure every single guest receives my wedding promo card.

Diamonds Are For Everyone

I love being able to use items off the tables when I perform, and even though I have this set up, if they are available on the tables, I will skip my props and use the ones that are scattered.

Effect:
The Magician has a card selected, remembered and lost back in the deck.
The spectator is asked to think of the selected card and the Magician makes a fist with his left hand.

The spectator is asked to hold out their hand, palm upwards and also to name their card, for example, the 4 of Diamonds, when the Magician turns over his fist 4 small diamonds fall out into the spectator's outstretched hand.

Required.
A ThumbTip

You will also require a small amount of the little diamond decorations that are scattered on the tables.

If the wedding does not have any of these table decorations you can easily buy them from ebay or amazon etc.

I bought 1000 in a medium size for around £20, and usually give away a few at each wedding.

For the routine you need to decide how many you want to produce, depending on size, I normally do a lesser number so for this example I would choose 2 or 3 diamonds.

Depending on the size you choose, you should be able to fit 3 of the medium size diamonds into a thumb tip.

You will also need a deck of cards.

Routine.

I place the diamonds into the thumb tip and have it in my thumb tip holder, which I will describe at the end of this effect. You can always use the little ticket pocket, which is the small pocket on the inside of your suit jacket.

I have the cards shuffled and then as I show the deck is mixed I move the desired force card to the top of the deck.

The easiest way to do this is, when you spot the card, cut the deck at that position and it will bring the force card to the top of the pack.

I now force the desired card onto the spectator, I use the classic force but you can use any force you feel comfortable with.

I ask the spectator to concentrate on the card and as they do this, I steal the thumbtip with the diamonds inside.

I ask the spectator to hold out their free hand, palm up as I make a fist around the thumbtip.

I can now turn my hand over and deliver the diamonds into the spectators hand.

I can now ask them to name their card and it will of course match the number of diamonds
I have just made appear.

Alternate Idea.
Another Idea for this is to have a blank faced card at the 2nd position from the top of the deck, (just below the force card).

After I have forced the card I take the card back and as I ask them to open their left hand palm up, I perform a top change and place the blank faced card face down on their hand.

They believe they have their card but as stated you have now given them the blank faced card.

Now I will ask them to name their card and when they have I ask them to turn over the card, they see the card is now blank.

I now produce the diamonds and place them into the spectators open palm.

Thoughts.
Simple direct magic with an easy to follow plot, this works well for any age and is well suited especially if they already have diamonds on the tables.

If they do have diamonds on the tables, I will normally steal some from the table as I am doing other things and then scatter them back afterwards.

Normally, weddings will have a much smaller diamond on the tables which means you can fit a lot more into a thumb tip for the revelation.

You can also take a small diamond and make it grow into a larger one for a bonus effect if desired.

Wayne's Thumbtip Holder.
This is a small holder that I started using back in the early 90's, it looks battered but it is never really seen and still works perfectly so I have never upgraded or updated it.

The thumbtip holder is actually a pen knife holder and is made of a soft nylon

material, although you can easily find a nice leather or vegan leather alternative.

The holder did have a flap on the top but on my version I have cut this off to

allow a quicker retrieval.

This attaches to my belt loop and it holds my thumbtip in an upright position.

Having a holder like this on your belt opens up the opportunity to perform a huge number of effects including producing difficult items like liquids and salt or sugar etc.

This idea came to fruition after watching the amazing David Williamson teach his salt to cup routine on his lecture dvd.

It also means I do not have to go into my pocket to retrieve the thumbtip before using it, and also when dumping the thumbtip after using it.

If you can find the right size and flexible enough material then this holder, when empty, will also hold a shot glass.

Wayne's Wizarding Wine

This is my main routine for weddings and one that I love to perform. Not only does it have layered, building moments of magic it also leaves the B&G with a souvenir that they are guaranteed to keep and remind them of their special day.

Effect;
The magician, That's you, performing magic at the top table, produces a full bottle of wine and presents it to the bride and groom.

Following this amazing production with a couple of other effects the magician concludes his performance with an impossible revelation and a gift that the Bride and Groom will keep forever.

Method:
The way this effect works requires a little set up and preparation and this starts at the time of booking.

The main revelation is that the bottle of wine, which is a normal bottle of wine, has been altered by adding a new personalised label to the bottle.

These labels can be purchased online at any number of places and a quick google search will generate a vast number of options.

This is one I got for a 30th birthday party and produced as a gift from her parents.

I get mine from ebay and they cost £3.75 with free postage but you can find many different designs etc for whatever purpose you require.

This routine has been through many trials and revamps.

It started as a simple bottle of wine production, at the time I was using a simple bottle holder I had purchased in a small magic shop in Barcelona called Magicus when I was living in Spain.

When I returned to the UK and the Splash Bottle gimmick was released I instantly upgraded to this.

In recent times I have upgraded my holdout again and now highly recommend the brilliant Prosecco Deluxe by proshow magic.

This amazing gimmick is first class, brilliantly made and available from Gary James at,

www.proshowmagic.co.uk/product/pro-secco

Then I added a personalised wine label and this was the first part of the new routine.

Do not underestimate the power this simple bottle carries though, when the B&G realise that the bottle of wine is personalised with their own names, this is enough to cause a real reaction that soon flies around the whole room.

It did not take me long to realise that by requesting a few small things on the bottle label, it opened up the possibilities of a few very smart revelations.

I have changed my labels over the years to include information such as the name of the place the B&G first had a first date or the where they met etc and to be honest these got great reactions but the way I do it now is the way I prefer.

The label is simple enough, it only carries three pieces of information on it and these are,

The name of the Bride and Groom.

The date of their wedding.

The two cards they will use in the anniversary waltz.

This bottle is loaded into the Prosecco gimmick and with the desired card ready to roll in the pack of cards I can now approach and perform for the Bride and Groom.

The routine.
I approach the top table and take out a large silk, from within the silk I now produce the bottle of wine.

I tell the B&G that this is a gift to them both but I DO NOT hand it to them, rather I place it onto the table in front of them with the label facing away from them.

At this point they assume that it is just a regular bottle of wine.

Now I offer to show them some special magic and start to perform my B&G set.

After I have completed the set and finished the anniversary waltz and I am preparing to leave the top table, I put my hand on the top of the bottle and I ask the B&G if they have enjoyed their day, if it has truly been a day to remember?

This is always met with smiles and beams and a confirmation that it has been and they will always remember the day.

I then inform them that it was my job to make sure that they had the best day, to see the real magic and give them memories of wonder and love and amazement.

Then, I draw attention to the bottle once again and as I hold the bottle by the top I gently start to turn the bottle so that they can see the label.

The realisation that their names are across the label will take a couple of seconds.

After the initial reaction I will also point out the date is their wedding date and also the names of their chosen cards.

This routine is normally the catalyst for the B&G to both hug me and thank me profusely and is always mentioned in after the day emails etc.

This is my signature routine for weddings and something I have not ever shared before in lectures or even talking to other magicians until I decided to include it in this book.

I hope you enjoy it as much as I have enjoyed performing it and get a lot of use and fun out of it.

The Horror Stories

Weddings are such a beautiful day, they are full of love and laughter, the joyous first steps of a new combined life and love story between 2 people dedicated to spending the rest of their lives together and maybe growing their family with children and pets.

Weddings are a day of laughter and I have a ton of wedding jokes,

My marriage was like a walk in the park.
Jurassic park.

I had a fairytale wedding.
Grimm

My love life is like a pack of cards.
First come the Hearts, then the Diamonds, now I am looking for a Club and a Spade.

However the truth is, not all wedding days are stories of fun and happiness and I have experienced my fair share of wedding day horrors.

I am going to share a couple of stories here to show you that no matter how bad your day is going, it's probably not as bad as these couples.

Horror Story 1.
The wedding had gone really well and I was booked to perform for an extra hour after the speeches when the evening guests were arriving and while they turned the room around from day to evening.

I had a cup of tea and was sat at the bar listening to the speeches, the Father of the Bride gave an emotional well written speech, then the Groom stood up and gave an equally great speech, and finally the Bestman, who started strong until he mentioned he had been in an secret affair with the bride, it sounded like a joke, then he shrugged his shoulders, said it was true, got out his phone and in front of everyone called himself a taxi and walked out.

Horror Story 2.
The chief Bridesmaid was the Bride's sister and had inserted herself into the running of the wedding day, she was overbearing and had caused a huge scene before the ceremony.

We got to the wedding breakfast, and no one had told the Bridesmaid that the B&G had switched the speeches from after the meal to before, and the Bridesmaid had a complete meltdown and punched the Groom, as she accused him of ruining the whole day.

She was removed and the day continued, but trying to get any atmosphere going was now three times as hard.

Horror Story 3.
I turned up to the wedding, I was booked to follow the speeches and into the evening reception, and was met by one of the groomsmen, he was in a mild state of panic and as I approached he called out to me and said,

"Are you the magician?"
"Yes", I said and he replied,
"Thank goodness, we have a bit of a situation and I need your help.

I calmed him down and he explained the issue.

The Bride's mother has smashed a glass in the face of the Groom's mother, the Bride's Mother has been arrested and the Groom's mother has been taken to hospital.

The Groom's father has waded in and grabbed the knife that was to be used to cut the cake and stabbed the Bride's father, they were also separated and the Groom's father was also arrested and the Bride's father has been taken to hospital.

He then said,

"The tension is quite high and we need you to get everyone laughing".

When I entered the room they had split the tables between the two sides of the dance floor, I approached the first table, and they were over the top nice to me.

When I started to cross the dance floor to entertain the first table of the other family, I was met by a huge gentleman who informed me that if I was entertaining "THAT" family then I was not welcome at their family tables.

"Fair enough", I said with a smile and went back to the first side and carried on with their tables, all of who responded enthusiastically to everything I did,

When I finished the first tables the Groom returned, thanked me and said I was good to go home.

It is not all doom and gloom.
It is important to remember though that these examples are at the extreme end of the spectrum, and for every horror story I have, I have a thousand amazing and beautiful memories to counter them.

"There is no remedy for love but to love more."
Henry David Thoreau

Wedding Jokes

I made my wife's dreams come true and we were married in a castle.
You sure wouldn't have known it from the look on her face as we were bouncing around.

My girlfriend is always stealing my t-shirts and sweaters... But if I take one of her dresses, suddenly "we need to talk".

My wife said, "You act like a detective too much. I want to split up." "Good idea," I replied. "We can cover more ground that way."

"I do," I said.
"I do," she said
"Agadoo-doo-doo" Black Lace said, and that was our wedding.

My wife just told me sex is even better when on holiday.
Not the kind of postcard I was expecting.

Apparently if your girlfriend or wife ever says "if anything happens to me, I want you to meet someone new."
"Anything" doesn't include getting stuck in traffic.

It is true that love is blind?
Because marriage is definitely an eye-opener.

My aunts used to come up to me at weddings, poking me in the ribs and cackling and telling me, "You're next!"
They stopped after I started doing the same thing to them at funerals.

It was an emotional wedding, even the cake was in tiers.

Marriages are made in heaven.
Then again, so are thunder, lightning, tornadoes, and hail.

I just saw two nuclear technicians getting married.
The bride was radiant, and the groom was glowing.

Do you know why the King of Hearts married the Queen of Hearts?
They were perfectly suited to each other.

Love is one long sweet dream, and marriage is the alarm clock.

Marriage is more than just a word, it is a sentence ... a life sentence.

My marriage was all about love, plain and simple.
She was plain and I am simple.

We married for better or for worse.
She could have done better, and I couldn't have done worse

Men are like buses.
They have spare tires and smell funny.

My new girlfriend works at a zoo, I think she may be a keeper.

Why should you never date a tennis player?
Because love means nothing to them.

Just went on a date with a welder.
The sparks were flying

My girlfriend is a tightrope walker, do you know how we met?
Online dating.

My girlfriend told me she was leaving me because I keep pretending to be a Transformer.
I said, "No, wait! I can change!"

My girlfriend left me because she couldn't handle my OCD.
I told her to close the door five times on her way out.

My wife and I often laugh about how competitive we are.
I laugh more though.

If I ever have a heart transplant, I'd want my ex's.
It's never been used.

Relationships are a lot like algebra.
Have you ever looked at your X and wondered Y?

They keep saying the right person will come along.
I think mine got lost.

My girlfriend just told me that she didn't care what she got for Christmas, as long as it had diamonds in it.
Looks like somebody's getting a pack of cards.

Wayne's Wedding Statement

This book has been a desire of mine to write for the last 10 years but I have put it off, mainly due to other projects such as other books or tricks.

In that time though I have been working and making my career by working at hundreds of weddings and learning and using the secrets, ideas and concepts in this book to push my career forward.

I love performing and I love weddings. The sense of fulfillment when you leave a wedding and you head home knowing you have had such an impact on the day fills me with joy and everytime it reminds me why I do what I do.

Weddings are not easy gigs, they take planning and there is a lot of responsibility on your part, you do not want to be the reason the Bride is in tears or the Groom is annoyed.

Magic is an art form, but it is also a gift, you have a fantastic gift that you can share with everyone around you and at a wedding you are enhancing the joy, wonder and magic of a beautiful day that is already filled with emotion and spectacle.

So now it is down to you to take the next step, get out there and start making a name for yourself as a wedding magician.

Remember it is not easy, but then again who wants to take the easy route.

So enjoy and also do not just do the magic, be the magic.

Thank you so much for purchasing and reading this book.
If you would like to read more by the Wayne Goodman please contact:
wayne@waynegoodman.co.uk

The Comedy Magicians Joke File vol 1 - 3.	The Complete Comedy Magicians Joke File.
Definitive Guide to Restaurant Magic.	The Expert at the Restaurant Table.
Weddings … I Do	Collection of Kings
The Joke File vol 1-3.	Plan, Prepare, Perform.
The Complete Joke File	Go Compere.
Parabellum	Maxims Primer
The Jedi Philosophy.	The Lean.
The Restaurant Course.	Remote Control.
Lord of the Bling.	Look Sharp.
Prism.	Clone.
Marked.	Asbo.
Sam the bell hog.	Time Traveller
WG Comedy Prediction.	Royal Brainwave.
421 Card.	Get the Joke
Cook with Charlee.	Amazing jokes for 8 - 10 year olds.

Or visit

www.waynegoodman.co.uk/shop